❀ It's Your World. ❀
What Are You Going to
Do with It?

Kids with a message can make sure our ~~pla~~ transmission. The more you learn, the more you can help others understand too.

How much do you know about the animal kingdom?

1. Pigeons can fly:
   a. As fast as a bicycle.
   b. As fast as a car.
2. Hens and their chicks start talking to each other:
   a. When the chicks are still inside the eggshells.
   b. Never! Chickens can't talk!
3. What do blue whales and rabbits have in common?
   a. They're both mammals.
   b. They both love Easter.
4. How many hearts does an earthworm have?
   a. One.
   b. Ten.

Answers:

1. b. Some pigeons can fly at speeds of fifty miles per hour!
2. a. Hens make at *least* eleven different peeps and clucks to talk to their babies as early as two days before the chicks hatch.
3. a. Blue whales are mammals and need to breathe air. Their blowholes are like our nostrils. Another fun fact: The blue whale's heart is the same size as a Volkswagen Rabbit!
4. b. Ten. And if you think that's impressive, consider this: The queen of a certain termite species can lay 40,000 eggs in just one day!

Turn the page for awesome reviews
from your favorite celebrities!

Your favorite stars speak out for

50 AWESOME WAYS KIDS CAN HELP ANIMALS

"An opportunity for parents and kids to learn together how to make the whole planet more humane. The lessons here will reverberate well beyond the reading of the book."

—Edie Falco

"This book helps kids put their good feelings into action and shows them how easy it is to be aware of animals around them and know exactly what to do to help animals in trouble. Full of games and activities for the entire family to do together—give it to your kids and let them teach you a thing or two!"

—Jennie Garth

"Inspiring! Exciting! Useful! Great lessons! Perfect for kids of all ages! This book celebrates a love for life and compassion for animals, a perfect combination."

—Summer Phoenix and Casey Affleck

"This is a compassionate and simple manuscript for animal-loving kids to live by. I read it, and my nine-year-old vegetarian animal rights activist daughter, Samia, read it. We both agree it is awesome!"

—Kathy Najimy, comedienne, and Samia Najimy Finnerty

"Ingrid Newkirk's writings are insightful, funny, and witty. It is a must-have book for every child in every classroom."

—Hailey Anne Nelson, young Roseanne Cash in *Walk the Line*

"I think it should be mandatory for everyone to read this book, kids and adults. Hopefully, fewer animals will suffer because of this book."

—Ridge Canipe, young Johnny Cash in *Walk the Line*

50 AWESOME WAYS KIDS CAN HELP ANIMALS

Fun and Easy Ways to Be a Kind Kid

INGRID NEWKIRK

WARNER BOOKS

BOSTON   NEW YORK

The information provided in this book is based on sources that the author believes to be reliable, and the author has attempted to verify its accuracy. All such information regarding individual products and companies is current as of March 2006.

Previously published as *Kids Can Save the Animals*
Copyright © 1991, 2006 by Ingrid Newkirk
All rights reserved.

Warner Books
Hachette Book Group USA
1271 Avenue of the Americas
New York, NY 10020
Visit our Web site at www.HachetteBookGroupUSA.com

Printed in the United States of America

First Edition: July 1991
First Revised and Updated Edition: November 2006
10 9 8 7 6 5 4 3 2 1

Warner Books and the "W" logo are trademarks of Time Warner Inc. or an affiliated company. Used under license by Hachette Book Group USA, which is not affiliated with Time Warner Inc.

Library of Congress Cataloging-in-Publication Data

Newkirk, Ingrid.
    50 awesome ways kids can help animals : fun and easy ways to be a kind kid / Ingrid Newkirk.—1st rev. and updated ed.
        p.   cm.
    Rev. ed. of: Kids can save the animals. c1991.
    Includes index.
    ISBN-13: 978-0-446-69828-3
    ISBN-10: 0-446-69828-8
    1. Animal welfare—Juvenile literature.   2. Humane education—Juvenile literature.   I. Title: Fifty awesome ways kids can help animals.   II. Newkirk, Ingrid. Kids can save the animals.   III. Title.
HV4708.N494   2006
179'.3—dc22   2006007677

Book design by Stratford Publishing Services, Inc.

. . . this is the time for thinking
Quite revisionary thoughts
About bats, dinosaurs and other creatures
Of weird and wonderful sorts.
—Ann Cottrell Free
No Room, Save in the Heart

This book is dedicated to all those who have thought
enough about animals to do something for them.

❀ Contents ❀

❀ Acknowledgments ❀

Thanks go to Maya Linden, who worked hard on this book, digging up facts, coming up with quizzes, throwing out bad jokes, and brainstorming for ideas with the wonderful PETA Kids educators, Patricia Trostle and Sangeeta Kumar.

Maya lives in the United States now, but she grew up in Australia, and when you hear how she grew up, you will see why she was a good choice to help put this book together.

Although her home was in a huge city, Melbourne, Maya often spent the weekend at an inner-urban sanctuary for animals called the Collingwood Children's Farm. There she and her sisters and friends would care for the animals. They'd muck out the pigs' stall, groom the horses, clean the chicken shed, and do the rounds of bottle-feeding baby goats and calves. Maya also adopted guinea pigs and enjoyed building wonderful palaces for them, complete with lots of platforms and ladders. Like Sangeeta, Maya was lucky enough to be raised as a vegetarian and so she never, ever ate animals. Her mom made the best "yummy vegan pizza and choc-mocha cakes," she says!

Patricia has a degree in elementary education and, as a "youth marketing specialist," she has spent eight happy years talking to kids and teachers, and making everything from lesson plans to zany animal costumes and classroom exercises for them (as well as telling them which of their favorite stars care about animals too!).

Patricia is the Queen of Educational Stuff That Kids Love and has helped create many of the freebies you'll read about in this book. She "test drives" the materials at teachers' conferences around the country and by asking kids their opinions about everything from the drawings to the competitions. The cats who supervise her work, Bonnie and Elisabeth, give her their opinions too!

Sangeeta is from Pakistan, and loves to share her knowledge of how animals are treated in Asia and around the world. She helped create the largest humane education initiative in U.S. history, a program used by over 60,000 teachers in the United States alone! She has spoken to thousands of students about animal protection and loves her job.

Sangeeta says, "What I love about humane education is that it will have a lasting impact on the generations to come. There is no doubt in my mind that if we are to have real change in our society, we will have to awaken the power of youth."

Other people who chipped in with enthusiasm to make this book a fun but educational part of kids' lives are Robyn Wesley, who puts together the children's animal magazine *Grrr!*; Meg Caskey, who is the glue in PETA's production department; and Matt Partridge, who is PETA's kids art specialist. Thanks also go to Sara Chenoweth, who was there to advise us on all things technical, and to Bruce Friedrich, Tal Ronnen, Brandi Valladolid, Daphna Nachminovitch, Ann Marie Dori, and Debbie Leahy for helping with campaign information. Tracy Reiman, Jay Kelly, and Angela Modzelewski were also great sources of wisdom.

As always, I owe a debt of gratitude to Mary Ann Naples, who put this book on the market, without which there is nothing; to Warner Books' Joann Davis and Colleen Kapklein, who helped get the original book going many years ago, and to Leila Porteous, who did the same for this edition. Thanks, everyone, for helping kids to help the animals!

❀ Special Note ❀
To Parents and Teachers
From the Author

In this book you will find suggestions for all sorts of things children can do to help their natural friends, the animals. Older generations, including my own, were shortchanged; most of us loved animals with all our hearts, yet most of us dissected a frog, dreamed of wearing a fur coat, and were persuaded not to think where our meals came from. Today's generation wants not just to be honest about what happens to the animals, but to make a difference. These kids are destined to teach us some excellent lessons. If you would like more detailed information on any topic in this book, please do not hesitate to write me personally at PETA, 501 Front St., Norfolk, VA 23510.

❀ Foreword for Kids ❀

—by Ricky Ullman

Cruelty to animals is much more prominent in our world than many of us think. Once you open your eyes to animal suffering, you begin to see so many things done to animals that are cruel and unnecessary.

Since I was five, I've had a dog named Zoe. She's a mutt: black lab and something else. She was a rescue dog and instantly became a part of our family. I remember bringing her home from the shelter—she sat on my lap on the ride home. She used to play with us kids in the backyard, in the sandbox, playing tag. She would actually push us around in a little red wagon with her front paws!

Unfortunately, I also remember having a neighbor who was very mean to his dog. We would hear him from our house, and it terrified me. My mom called the animal rights "police" and reported him. After that, I don't think it happened again—thankfully!

But so many other animals in our own country *are* being abused, hurt, and killed. This suffering can be stopped, too, by anybody who cares enough to take action.

Animal testing is something that I find very wrong. If a product might be unsafe for humans to use, then there is no reason to test it on other living beings. Education is another area in which animals are hurt and killed, even though there are now so many cruelty-free alternatives. I think it is important for students to learn as much as possible, but there is a line that is sometimes crossed. I believe that students should have the right to choose whether or not they want to dissect animals and not to be ridiculed for showing compassion in the classroom.

Right now, *you* can really make a big difference! You can write letters, talk to people, and lead by example. By showing people that you care, others will start to care too. This book will show you the many reasons why animals need your help today and give you at least 50 ways to help make sure that the future will be cruelty free for all living creatures.

Thanks for caring and for doing something to help!

❀ Foreword for Parents ❀
—by Summer Phoenix and Casey Affleck

Summer:

As a parent, I look back on my childhood at lessons I learned and how I was raised, and I think about which of those lessons I would like to pass on to my own child.

What inspired my family, and what inspires me, is the choice to be non-violent. There are many studies showing that children who are raised to care about animals tend to become more considerate in their relations with other human beings.

I have cared about animals my whole life. This has a lot to do with how I was raised. I was pretty lucky in that way: By the time I was born (I'm the fifth of five children), my entire family had become vegetarian. A little later, they decided to try not to take or use anything from animals. So I have been a vegan all my life!

From my mother, from my studies, and from my own experience, I know that a plant-based diet is the optimum diet for health. That's why Casey and I have raised Indiana to leave animals off his plate and taught him active kindness from day one. Like all caring parents, we want him to grow up good and strong—inside and out!

I think the best and only way to reach someone is to be true to yourself. It really comes down to my love for life and my desire to extend that love and compassion by raising my child to respect and care about all the animals of the world.

Casey:

I am a vegan because I believe that animals have souls and experience pain. I am a vegan for my own well-being as well. I don't eat any animal products because I don't believe they are good for me physically, emotionally, or spiritually. Eating vegan over the past ten years has made me feel more energetic and balanced. It is a substantial commitment of love to oneself and to all other living creatures.

Helping kids develop into loving, healthy adults is something that every parent wants to do. One way to do that is by encouraging their natural affection for animals. We made the decision to raise our son vegan because we believe that it is the best choice we can make for him until he is able to choose for himself.

I hope others will do the same!

© Summer Phoenix/Casey Affleck 2006

🐾 Introduction 🐾

When I was about eight years old, I left the little English town of Ware ("Where?" my new friends would ask), left my school and everyone I knew, and headed off, with my parents, to a very different life thousands of miles away in India.

From that moment on, everything was different. The ocean liner we took on our two-week voyage was many stories tall, and when I first started walking up the gangplank, I felt so frightened that my knees wobbled. It didn't seem possible that such a huge, heavy skyscraper of a ship could float! That first night, everyone became ill from the motion of the waves, and I wished I could go home again. Out in the open ocean there were animals I had never seen before: flying fishes, giant turtles, and manta rays. Dolphins leaped out of the water, chasing the ship's bow. At night there was only the light of the moon, no land or other ships to be seen. During the day there was only water, stretching from horizon to horizon.

When we arrived in Bombay, big birds called kites circled in the sky. There were even vultures and parrots to watch. Camels, bullocks, and men pulled carts through the streets. Everything we ate was odd: fruits called lichees and guavas, figure-eight candies called *gulabjamun*, spicy curries, and little pastries cut into triangles and fried in vats of oil on the street. Some people spoke English, but most spoke one of the many Indian languages. It was peculiar to hear everyone chatting but not have any idea what they were saying. When I spoke, Indian children would giggle at me. On the train, my father began to teach me to count—*ek, do, tin, char*—and how to say "please" and "thank you" in Hindi.

Sometimes I think my experience must have been a little bit like what animals go through in today's world. We don't speak their language, and perhaps we laugh at them sometimes when they are trying to tell us something serious.

Our clothes, our cars, our foods, the things we do that seem ordinary to us, must be very strange to them. Other-than-human beings look terrific in the feathers, fur, and hair they were born with! In their own homelands, they eat well and stay healthy on natural foods, like nuts, berries, seeds, fruits, and vegetables. To keep happy, they play chase, sing, sunbathe, and invent simple games. Can you imagine a dog buying a party dress, a cow ordering out for pizza, or a bat playing a video game?

Sometimes animals from faraway countries are forced to leave their friends behind, just as I had to. I was very lucky because my parents came with me. Whenever I was frightened, they explained what was happening and that everything would be all right. My trip was comfortable, too. No such luck for the animals. Those captured in South America for a New York pet shop or torn from their mothers' arms in Africa for an American zoo can be crammed into a small cage in the hold of a ship or smuggled—even upside down—in the false linings of suitcases. Many die on their voyages, and those who survive find a life that is often lonely and very sad. No one speaks their language, and they are often ignored or misunderstood.

When you think about it, what many animals go through is pretty awful, but there's no point in being glum when we can easily make things better. There are tons of things we can do to help animals and to make sure they do enjoy life: things we can make and buy, things we can say, ways we can stick up for the animals just by knowing their likes and dislikes and by making sure other people get to know them, too.

Alex Pacheco and I formed People for the Ethical Treatment of Animals in 1980 to let people know what animals go through in our world and to encourage everyone to pitch in and make the animals' plight better. Today there are over 1 million PETA Kids and PETA adult members speaking up for all other-than-human beings. That's pretty exciting!

As you read this book, you will probably think of lots of other ideas that aren't in here, because there are as many ways to help animals as there are kids in the world. I'd love to hear *your* ideas, so please write to me at PETA and let me know what *you* are doing to save the animals. *Good luck!*

—*Ingrid Newkirk*

50 AWESOME WAYS
KIDS CAN
HELP ANIMALS

CHAPTER 1

Do Unto Others . . .

To understand any living being you must creep within and feel the beating of his heart.

—W. Macneile Dixon

Be your dogs' angel. Play with them . . . take them for nice long walks . . . don't ever chain them.

—David Boreanaz,
Angel in *Angel* and *Buffy the Vampire Slayer*

Animals have feelings, just as you and I do. Just like us, they feel the heat and cold, the sun and rain. Just like us, they enjoy a comfortable place to live, good food, and loving attention. They miss you when you are away, and they remember things that have happened to them. We think of some animals as our friends. Others we may think of as dangerous, and others we hardly think of at all. But all animals, from the family dog to the tiniest mouse, are like us: living, feeling beings. We can learn more about how animals experience life by trying to better understand their needs and their feelings.

Did You Know?

🐾 When Princess Beatrix of Holland was a child, she forgot one day to feed her dog. The next morning she was served no breakfast, on the orders of her father, Prince Bernhard. (What lesson do you think she learned?) The phrase *in the doghouse* means "in disgrace." This says a lot about how some people care for their dog's living space.

🐾 Stars of Fox Network's *The O.C.*, Adam Brody (Seth) and Rachel Bilson (Summer), are proud parents of a puppy named Penny Lane, adopted from a rescue center in Los Angeles. She is now a first-rate cuddle-pup who sleeps on Adam's bed—"she snores so loud," he told *Teen People*.

🐾 Most other-than-human beings have better-developed senses than people. A bloodhound's sense of smell is roughly 2 million times as sensitive as ours, so paint, cigarette smoke, air "fresheners," and cooking smells can really get to them. See how safely you can bring to domesticated animals as many of the pleasures of their natural lives, the fun and fulfilling things, like hopping, flying, splashing, jumping, and playing in the grass and trees, that their free-roaming relatives get to do.

🐾 When *Teen Vogue* asked *One Tree Hill* heartthrob Chad Michael Murray what specifically about his fellow castmate Sophie Bush he was drawn to, Chad said it was her big heart. "She took in a stray dog with seven puppies, which was a little bit of a nightmare since we already had five dogs, but I loved her for it." The pair were so devoted to helping animals that they didn't let a little thing like a honeymoon get

THEY SAID IT!

Here's what some of our fave celebs say about their animal companions:

"My animals are my life! They remind me always of unconditional love and to just be in the moment."
—Christina Applegate, *PETA Celebrity Cookbook*

"When I feel like playing, they are always willing to play. . . . If I'm in a bad mood after a game, I know my dogs will always bring me up."
—Adrian Klemm, New England Patriots offensive lineman, on his dogs, *USA Today*

"'I am at his service,' she says of her cat, Playdough. 'Whatever he wants me to do is what I do.'"
—Halle Berry, *People Magazine*

in the way of their support of their four-legged friends—they were spotted attending an animal-adoption fair the day after their wedding.

What You Can Do

Keep a journal about the dog or cat or gerbil in your own home or in the home of a friend or relative. Watch whenever you can—being sure not to disturb his or her normal habitat or routine—and note how much time this animal friend spends doing different things. What signs does she or he make to display feelings, just as you might? How does his or her behavior change as the things around him or her change? How would you feel in his or her place in different situations? You might imagine how your dog experiences a walk in the park ("I'm free, I'm free! Ooh, the smells! Oh, no, let's not go back inside so soon"), or what your cat thinks when she sees you preparing her dinner (Do you think they believe we go out hunting during the day and come home in the evening to share what we have found?).

Cats and Dogs

As a cat and/or dog guardian, there are lots of things you can do for your animal friend. Since animals in our lives can't turn on a tap to get a drink or drive themselves to the vet, it is up to you to make sure you:

- 🐾 Give them fresh water in a very clean bowl every single day.
- 🐾 Let them sleep inside with you or in a safe, snug shelter. They should have a soft, dry bed to keep them off the drafty floors and should never sleep outside when it's cold!
- 🐾 Give them a variety of healthy foods they enjoy. (Some dogs adore steamed broccoli and carrots. Some cats like chickpeas and melon. Do some taste tests as long as it isn't chocolate or cheese or other foods that are dangerous for non-humans.)

When they're out in the world, dogs have to follow all sorts of rules. This is funny sign for dogs (and their companions!) from North Vancouver:

Attention Dog Guardians

Pick up after your dogs. Thank you.

Attention Dogs

Grrrrr, bark, woof. Good dog.

District of North Vancouver. Bylaw 5981-11(i)

So when at home, let your dog be a playtime rebel and enjoy a bark-a-thon once in a while—a dog's gotta have some freedom to be a *happy* dog 'cause no one likes taking orders 24/7, not even people in the Marine Corps!

- Allow them plenty of playtime with you and other household and neighborhood companions.
- Give them plenty of chances to relieve themselves (at least four to five times each day and whenever they ask you to be let out, of course). If you want to really feel what it's like not to be able to "go," put yourself on exactly the same schedule as your dog and see if you could do that without feeling awful!
- Keep the cat's litter box or yard very, very clean (I won't ask you to imagine what that would be like if you had to put yourself in their paws!). The fact is that, nowadays, with dogs and cars and strangers about, cats should be kept indoors unless you are out there with them, keeping an eye on their safety.
- Teach the animals you share your home with the rules, using great patience and kindness, especially because they are trying to understand human language and human wants and we don't speak a word of their lingo. They should never be hit or scolded, as you know. Some humane societies have dog-training and cat-care booklets you can get for free.
- Feed them before you sit down to eat. Clearly, it's never polite to eat in front of anyone who hasn't already been served! When they're finished, say, "All gone," and make an "empty hands" signal with upturned palms, followed by a pat, so they won't expect food while you're eating. Oh, and they can't help it if they drool—that's a reflex!
- Make sure their collars are the right size. (Three of your fingers should fit under it.) Check it often, especially if your companion is still growing, or your pet could be quietly choking!
- Gently groom your friends every day if they need it. They should get brushed and combed and their coat checked for

fleas and ticks. Powdered brewer's yeast and garlic in their food can free them from harsh flea powders, sprays, and flea collars. A flea comb catches fleas in its teeth so your companions won't have to use theirs.

🐾 Give signs that your friends are loved often, like a friendly word or two, a scratch behind the ears, kisses, and treats.

Birds

Birds shouldn't be kept in homes, as they normally live in large flocks (meaning that they love to play with many other birds) and, as you know, they have wings so that they can fly! That means a lone bird in a cage is a sad sight. Parrots may even pluck out their own feathers when they are unhappy or stressed; some birds will rock back and forth endlessly as if dreaming of the outdoors and their bird friends, which they probably are. So make sure that any birds in your care have, at the very least:

🐾 One bird companion (from a sanctuary, if possible, never a pet shop because then they breed more and more and . . .)

🐾 Room to fly about in, such as a whole room or an outside aviary

🐾 Windows (to see out of—not go out of—that's too dangerous for them!)

🐾 Lots of perches that are big enough for them to wrap their feet around, just so their toenails touch

🐾 A seed dish always full of food (not hulls—the outer casing—which they tidily spit back into their dishes)

🐾 Something to sharpen their beaks on, such as a heavy, non-splintering piece of wood

🐾 Fresh fruits, fresh vegetables (carefully washed in case of insecticides or other chemicals and waxes), and clean water

🐾 Gravel (to help them digest their food)

🐾 A separate bowl of water to splash and bathe in, as well as to drink (some birds love a mist spray)

🐾 Toys (parakeets love measuring spoons) and gentle feather stroking

And make sure no one turns on a self-cleaning oven; the fumes can cause serious breathing problems for birds!

Rodents

Gerbils, guinea pigs, hamsters, rats, and mice should have:

🐾 A private space they can call their own, like upside-down boxes with holes cut in them
🐾 A clean, comfortable cage (a metal tray floor covered with newspaper sheets makes the best floor—wire mesh is quite painful to stand and walk on, and wood is hard to clean)
🐾 A cage large enough so they can scamper around (store-bought cages are ever so tiny—write to PETA to learn how to make a more suitable cage)
🐾 Things to climb and play in, like paper towel rolls, shelves, and old socks
🐾 An exercise wheel and tummy tickles with your little finger
🐾 Things to chew on, like tree branches or other hard, chemical-free wood, to help keep their teeth in good shape
🐾 Raisins and other food treats hidden in the cage

Rodents' cages should be cleaned at least once a week (more often if you imagine yourself small enough to live in there and think, "Pfew!"). And your small friends will love some supervised time outside of their cage every single day, although, before taking them out, search the room and floor boards to make sure there are no openings they can squeeze into and get stuck or lost.

Here's a tip: If you have both males and females, keep them in separate cages so you don't end up with a tribe of small animals. Female rodents can live nicely together, except for hamsters, who really do prefer to be alone. Most male rodents will fight, and no one wants that.

Rabbits

Rabbits love to be inside, just as cats do, although they'll let you know by stamping their feet if you are doing something they don't approve of. If you have rabbits who are kept outside, check that their hutch is totally dog proof and weatherproof and is raised on legs at least two feet off the ground. The hutch should have:

- A large screened outdoor area for stretching out and fresh air
- A snug nest box of solid wood
- Lots of hay for burrowing
- Roofing shingles attached on the outside of the box to protect it from bad weather

Here's a tip: Avoid bringing rabbits in and out of the house if the air-conditioning or heat are on, since rabbits are very sensitive to dampness and changes in temperature. Be sure to switch the hutch from outdoors to indoors before cold weather comes and if you see bunny tilting his head or scratching his ears as if they hurt, take him to the vet as fast as you can. If you have small caged animals, put a star by the things in this chapter you'd like to start doing to improve their lives.

How Do You Rate?

Take this quick quiz and find out how much of a friend you are to animals:

1. It is almost summer and your cat starts to shed her winter fur. It gets all over the sofa, her favorite hangout. You decide to:
   a. Hit her and scold her whenever she hops up on the sofa, then lock her outside for a time.
   b. Comb and stroke her carefully every day to rid her of loose hair and cover the sofa with an old sheet for however long it takes.

   c. Ban her from the sofa room for a few weeks but make her an alternative bed with cushions in the garage.

2. You've only had your bird for a few weeks when he becomes quiet and won't touch his food much. You decide:
   a. He is easier to handle when he is quiet—and you'll save money on birdseed if he doesn't eat.
   b. To find him a companion from a sanctuary so that he's not lonely anymore, buy or make him some new toys, and let him out to fly around the room at least once a day so he doesn't get bored.
   c. To let him out of his cage once a week to fly around part of the room.

3. You have just been given a tame rat. When you get her home, you:
   a. Release her somewhere in your house, near where the cat sleeps.
   b. Ask your dad to help you build a big comfortable cage for her, with ladders, exercise wheels, and a private sleeping box filled with cozy old socks. Then you set about researching all the foods rats love to eat.
   c. Find an old birdcage in the shed and put her in that, with some shredded newspaper and food pellets, and go back to watching TV.

Mostly a's There's an animal emergency in your house! You're not totally aware of how to care for animals in the way they need, so sometimes you cause them harm. You need to keep right on reading, starting with this book! Then your cat—and every other animal in the world—is guaranteed to think very highly of you.

Mostly b's Congratulations! You're one super-sensitive and totally kind kid. You're aware of how fragile animals are and how they need to be cared for, and your animal pals love you for it. Share your caring ways with friends and family—most of all, keep it up!

Mostly c's Here's the good news: you're halfway to being the compassionate person you could be. You know what you need to do to care for animals, but the bad news is that you don't always follow through with it. Keep reading and learning about animals' needs, and you'll definitely get there!

Check It Out

- Make a list of everything you can do to make life great for each animal in your household. Tape the list where you can check it every day. This way, you won't forget they're depending on you to look out for them, always!
- If you have hamsters, other rodents, birds, or rabbits, write to PETA at 501 Front St., Norfolk, VA 23510, or log on to www.petakids.com for some the great tips on keeping your best animal buddies happy.

CHAPTER 2

Don't Pester the Pigeons

Pretty pigeons
On the ground and in the trees
When they're chased and yelled at
They get shaky knees.
—Jessica Hubbard, age eight

Can you imagine sitting in the park, picnicking with friends, eating your sandwich or trying to sleep, when all of a sudden people run right through your picnic and start chasing you? Sounds crazy, or at least extremely rude, doesn't it?

Well, many parents watch little kids do exactly those sorts of things to pigeons, starlings, and other birds who are resting peacefully on the grass or eating seeds or crumbs. Some parents don't give such behavior a second thought, and some kids think it's a hoot to watch the pigeons scurry away or have to abandon their activities—or their naps—to fly out of reach. It's easy to see that the birds aren't having any fun while this is going on. Their hearts are probably racing a mile a minute. There are lots of birds, like geese, ducks, and starlings, who also need help. Read on to find out who they are and why they need you.

6 Things You Never Knew about Pigeons

Surprise your family with these funky facts on our flying friends:

1. Pigeons can fly very fast. In fact, some can fly at speeds of 50 miles per hour and cover 600 miles in one day!
2. An adult female is called a hen, and when her babies are learning to eat they are called peepers or squeakers.
3. Adult pigeons have better eyesight than humans because they can see all colors, as well as ultraviolet light (which we can't), and can memorize as many as 300 photographs and tell them all apart.
4. Pigeons never complain about their dinner—they have only 37 taste buds, while you have 9,000!
5. When it comes to drinking, you've got something in common: pigeons suck up water by using their beaks like straws! They have also demonstrated that they can associate a glass of water with the ocean.
6. Pigeons can live until they are fifteen years old, and once pigeons fall in love and settle down with a mate, they stay together for life.

Did You Know?

🐾 The pigeons we see in cities today are a kind of dove called a rock dove. They were brought to the United States from Europe by early settlers. Since doves are a universal symbol of peace, you'd think that people would treat pigeons with lots of respect!

🐾 Starlings were brought to the United States in 1890 by a man who loved William Shakespeare's work. Since Shakespeare wrote about starlings in one of his plays, the traveler thought the United States wouldn't be complete without them.

🐾 Squirrels hang out in parks, too. Like pigeons and starlings, they live mostly in the trees, drink from fountains, perhaps, and look for nuts and leftovers. All these beings have as much (or more) right to be there as we do because humans cut down the forests where they used to live, so they should be left in peace when we're sharing their space for fun.

🐾 At least one goose has saved a little girl's life. The girl's mother looked out the farmhouse window and saw that the goose had the toddler's dress in his bill and was pulling back hard. When the mother went outdoors to investigate, she found that her daughter had been about to tumble over the edge of an embankment when the goose grabbed her dress to pull her back.

🐾 Every summer, PETA's Wildlife Division receives about a million—well, a lot of—complaints from people most upset to learn that their city has hired the U.S. Department of Agriculture and Wildlife Services to round up and kill thousands of the Canada geese who, with nowhere to go anymore, have started to live year-round in public parks and on golf courses. In summer geese shed their feathers, and while they grow new ones they can't fly. This means the birds can't flee from danger, and, knowing this, wildlife controllers herd them into crates and usually kill them. That's no way to treat visitors from Canada!

What You Can Do

🐾 If you see little kids chasing pigeons, driving ducks, or startling starlings, try to talk to them—gently. It's not their fault that no one has ever pointed out to them that it's wrong to disturb, harass, or frighten birds or other animals. Let them know that pigeons don't mind being watched, from a distance, but that it scares them to be chased.

🐾 Adults, too, may never have thought of their children's actions from the pigeons' point of view, so if the pigeon chaser is too young to understand, ask the parent or guardian to please give the pigeons a break.

🐾 When you visit a big park with nature trails, resist the urge to leave the trails. These trails are like a street out in front of people's homes. When you go off the beaten path, you risk invading the privacy of animals who consider the park their living room and bedroom!

🐾 If you see a duckling or a group of ducklings walking or swimming alone without their mother, on land or on water, chances are they've been orphaned. To be sure, scan the area close by to see if there are any female ducks in the area, with or without ducklings. If none can be found, pick them up gently, place them in an animal carrier or a box, and keep the carrier or box in a warm and quiet place until you can get them to a nearby licensed wildlife rehabilitator for care.

🐾 If you see a mother duck and her ducklings on the side of the road, give them a hand by getting an adult to help stop traffic for a minute or two. Then gently herd the family across the street. Usually the mother duck is looking for water, so if you know of a nearby lake, pond, stream, or creek, gather the ducklings into a box or bucket (watch out, they can leap like little frogs!) and slowly walk to the water. Mom will follow you wherever you go with them, but be sure to walk slowly so she can keep up with you. Once you reach the water, release the ducklings, step way out of the way, and watch your rescue efforts pay off!

Check It Out

🐾 Call your local Department of Recreation and Parks (directory assistance at 411 will have the number) to find out if a park ranger can take your class on a tour of a park near you. A park ranger can point out different species of plants and animals living in the park—there are probably a lot more than you would think!

🐾 PETA, along with other animal groups, has provided city and county officials with information on humane ways to live with geese, but not all have scrapped plans to kill them. If you learn that the Canada geese in your local parks are being captured, write to your local Department of Agriculture and Wildlife Services and ask them to adopt a Canada goose–control program that everyone can live with, including the geese! There's a list of addresses at www.aphis.usda.gov/ws.

🐾 For more facts about saving geese (which would make a great school paper), click on to the Geese Peace page at www.geesepeace.org. You can also write to them at 6405 Lakeview Dr., Falls Church, VA 22041.

CHAPTER 3

Try It, You'll Like It

How would you feel if a cow ate you?
Caught you and bopped you,
And chopped you in two,
Fried you or broiled you or put you in the stew,
With carrots, potatoes, and an onion or two?
So sometime at dinner when you're starting to chew,
Put down your steak and ponder this through,
How would you feel if a cow ate you?

—Pete Traynor

Most of us grow up eating animals and not even realizing where meat comes from and how it gets to our plates. When we find out, it's usually a shock!

Nowadays, there are tons of vegetarians: people who won't eat animals because they care about animals, their own health, and the environment. Some people are vegans (pronounced VEE-guns). They don't eat any animal products, including eggs, milk, and cheese.

THEY SAID IT!

Here's what some of your fave celebs have to say about eating animals:

"When you dig a little below the surface what you find out is really disturbing and it makes veganism seem like the only option really. I can't even conceive of going back to eating animals at all."
—Mickey Madden, Maroon 5

"I get a proud feeling every time I'm in a restaurant or every time I'm out somewhere and I say 'No. I don't eat meat.' It's a pretty good feeling!"
—Benji Madden, Good Charlotte

"My son said, 'I'm really concerned about my health and about the health of the planet, and I'm going to go vegan.' And so it made me think, 'Well, wow! Maybe I should be cutting out cheese from my diet, maybe I should be thinking about dairy products and eggs.' So it was the big step my son took that helped me take the next step."
—Michael Franti, Spearhead

"I have been a vegetarian for 10 years and I went vegan four and half years ago. I just realized how disproportionate it was to kill a cow so somebody could eat lasagna!!"
—Alexis Desolneux, BMX rider

Did You Know?

🐾 The average American will eat 21 cows, 1,400 chickens, 12 pigs and 14 sheep in his or her lifetime.

- Most pigs, chickens, and other animals bred, raised, and killed for the dinner table have rotten lives. Although pictures on fast-food packages show them having a great time in the outdoors, they don't live that way anymore. Instead, almost all animals are raised inside crowded sheds, usually unable to turn around because there is so little room. Their babies are taken away from them almost as soon as they are born, which means they are never allowed to play, stretch, or feel the sunlight.

- Studies have shown that killing animals to eat kills us, too! The top diseases in the United States are heart disease, cancer, and stroke—all of them linked to eating meat. The good news is that a person's chance of getting these diseases when they get older are very small if they stop eating animals early in life.

- When land is used to raise animals instead of crops, precious water and soil are lost, trees are cut down to make land for grazing or factory farm sheds, and chemicals are used to fatten up the animals quickly and then end up in streams and in the earth.

- An area of rainforest the size of seven football fields is destroyed every minute to make room for grazing cattle. But each vegetarian saves one acre of trees every year—so it's not just the animals we might eat who are saved, but all the forest animals and trees get to live too!

- Most large cafés (and lots of smaller ones too) carry soy milk and are happy to use it in your drink if you ask them to. Next time you're ducking out of the winter cold for a steamy hot chocolate, make sure you ask for soy—and if the café doesn't have it, suggest they start!

- Many of the popular fast-food chains also carry good vegetarian options so you won't starve on the next road trip or be left out of lunch at the mall. Try Ruby Tuesday, Taco Bell, Johnny Rockets, or Subway, who all have tasty options suitable for vegans.

- After starring in the movies *Babe* and *Babe 2*, actor James Cromwell, who plays Farmer Hoggit, decided to stop eating all animal products. Get your friends together and arrange a DVD night where you watch the *Babe* movies or *Chicken Run* (a cartoon about hens who escape from a factory farm). See how many still want to eat real ham and biscuits or bacon afterwards!

- J. H. Kellogg, the man who started the Kellogg's cereal company, was a vegetarian. He used to say, "I don't eat anything with a face!"

- Ex-Beatle Paul McCartney and his beloved late wife Linda "went veggie" because they love the lambs and sheep on their farm and would rather see them die of old age than be baked in the oven. They became animal rights activists and raised all of their kids vegetarian, including Stella, a famous fashion designer who has her own cruelty-free clothing label and fragrance.

- Dave Scott, the only athlete ever to win the grueling Iron-man Triathlon more than once (he has won it at least six times!), is a vegetarian—and so is world-famous hurdler Edwin Moses. They're joined by other veg athletes like Ricky Williams (NFL); pro skaters Ed Templeton, Laban Pheidias, and Jen O'Brien; BMX biker Taj Mihelich; Anthony Peeler (NBA Grizzlies); John Salley (NBA Lakers); Peter Brock (Australian car racer); Carey Hart (motocross rider—who's also singer P!nk's husband!); and Brian Conley (champion surfer).

- All of these great celebs are also vegetarians: Alicia Silverstone, Josh Hartnett, Avril Lavigne, Jonathan Taylor Thomas, Natalie Portman, Tobey Maguire, Gwyneth Paltrow, Kristen Bell, Mya, Thora Birch, Prince, Dan Castellaneta (he's the voice of Homer Simpson), Samuel L. Jackson, Benji Madden, Joaquin Phoenix (and the rest of his family), Eddie Vedder, David Duchovny, Anthony Kiedis, Common, Mos Def, Amber Tamblyn, Alyssa Milano, Carrie Underwood, and Joss Stone. To stop guessing which other celebrities are vegan or vegetarian, just take a look at www.famousveggie.com

- You can get all the protein you need from vegetables, soy products, nuts, rice, wheat, potatoes, and beans. Vegetarians save their health while they save animals.

- A lot of people can't digest milk, and drinking it causes all kinds of problems—from runny noses to ear infections! Soy milk tastes great and is much better for a human being than cow's milk. (You can buy soy milk at most health food stores and some supermarkets.) The vanilla and chocolate varieties taste especially good and usually aren't any more fattening than the regular flavor. Elephants, giraffes, bulls, elk, rhinoceroses, moose, and gorillas are all vegetarians—more living proof that you can grow big and strong without eating meat! As for calcium, the best kind your body needs is in green, leafy veggies, orange juice, and nuts. And lots of soy milks are fortified with calcium, too.

What You Can Do

Being a vegetarian can cost less than eating meat, makes mealtimes interesting because there are so many new foods to try, and shows you have a big heart. You can start slowly rather than stop all at once, or you can switch your diet overnight. Here are just some ideas of what to eat instead of pigs, cows, chickens, and lambs:

🐾 Try tofu! It sounds like "toad food," but it's an amazing people food that has been eaten in China for over two thousand years. Now it's here in the United States. Don't try it raw or you'll never try it again. Crumbled tofu can be scrambled with onions, tomatoes, and turmeric, garlic, salt, and pepper for breakfast. You can put it in the blender with fresh fruit or lemon juice to make a creamy dip. It can be baked in casseroles; breaded and fried; blended and cooked in pies (like pumpkin and coconut cream); mixed with seasonings, made into patties, and fried for tofu "burgers"; and frozen, thawed, sliced, smothered in barbecue sauce, and cooked on the grill to fulfill every barbecue lover's dream. It is full of protein and iron.

🐾 Baked potatoes (including sweet potatoes) are easy to make and fun to eat! If you have a microwave, you can bake a potato in only seven or eight minutes, depending on its size. Then you can put all kinds of good things on it: margarine, Bac*Os (made from vegetables, of course!), ketchup, barbecue sauce, Italian salad dressing, or tofu "sour cream" from a company called Tofutti (or make your own with half a pound of soft tofu blended at high speed with $1/4$ cup of oil, 1 tablespoon lemon juice, $1 1/2$ teaspoons sugar, and $1/2$ teaspoon salt).

🐾 Use your noodle! Go Italian with great easy-to-make spaghetti. Cook some pasta and pour your favorite (non-meat) spaghetti sauce over it—presto! Try different shapes, colors, and flavors of noodles. At health food stores and some grocery stores you can find whole-wheat noodles, spinach noodles, noodles made with tomatoes or artichokes, noodles in different shapes and sizes, and even noodles that look like poodles!

🐾 Did you know that broccoli contains more calcium per calorie than any other food? (*Moo*-ve over, milk!) Vegetables like broccoli, cauliflower, kale, Brussels sprouts, and spinach taste great even though they're good for you. If you don't like these vegetables straight off the stove top, right out of the microwave, or raw, use your imagination to spice them up!

Dill, garlic, curry, onion salt, or Italian salad dressing can add a lot of zip to plain vegetables. Some people like barbecue sauce on their cauliflower, and many people put a little lemon juice on their spinach. Try all kinds of things until you find what you like. Green, leafy vegetables are a great source of calcium, iron, and vitamin C.

🐾 After a feel-good veggie meal, spoil yourself with a veggie dessert! Don't think that because you're vegan you'll miss out on all the awesome flavors. Soy Delicious makes rich, non-dairy ice creams with names like Chocolate Peanut-Butter Zig Zag and Mocha Almond Fudge, and another vegan ice-cream company, Temptation, has flavors like Peach Cobbler, Mint Chip, and Chocolate Chip Cookie Dough. You can find out more at www.welovesoy.com. For a complete list, take a look at all the vegan meat- and dairy-free foods and vegetarian ready-made meals listed at the back of this book—you'll be overwhelmed by the variety!

🐾 Borrow a vegetarian cookbook from the library and throw your meat burgers to the wind; try a whole bunch of different recipes until you've found your new favorites.

🐾 Volunteer to cook dinner once a week for your family, and provide them with great veggie meals. If your family is not vegan or vegetarian, ask if they're willing to eat vegan one or two nights each week because you love them, want them to live forever, and it's an adventure you can have together.

🐾 Why not host a vegan dinner party or sleepover for all your friends? Ask them what their top rated animal-based foods are, then make up a cruelty-free menu with all the delicious substitutes you can find. It might look something like this:

Appetizer: Boca Chick'n Nuggets with spicy peanut dipping sauce

Main Course: Homemade pizza with Vegi-Deli Pepperoni and melted Tofutti cheese slices or spaghetti with Yves Veggie "Neatballs" and tomato sauce.

Dessert: Tofutti Blueberry Cheesecake and Soy Dream French Vanilla ice cream.

🐾   After dinner, suggest a game of cards using the animal-rights-themed deck from PETA. The reverse side of these cards shows fun cartoons and serious tags like a chicken saying "I am not a nugget," so you can get the message across 52 times! Check them out at www.petamall.com.

How Do You Rate?

Take this gory true-or-false test and see if you know what you're really eating:

1. Red candy coloring is sometimes made from crushed beetle shells.

2. Jell-O gelatin crystals contain the boiled hooves, noses, and bones of cows.

3. Hot dogs sometimes contain meat from dogs.

4. Pretzels are sometimes glazed with animal pee.

5. Buffalo wings are actually the ribs of wild baby buffalos.

6. Some margarine is made with oils taken from whales' heads.

Answers: 1. True; 2. True; 3. False; 4. True; 5. False; 6. True

Check It Out

🐾   Flip to the end of this book, to Appendix A, "Recipes for Kids Who Care," for some tasty, easy recipes you can make yourself. Try cooking from these recipes for a bake sale fund-raiser, holiday pot luck, or birthday surprise meal for friends, your family—or just for fun!

🐾 Contact the Vegetarian Resource Group. Check out the Web site at www.vrg.org or write to VRG, P.O. Box 1463, Baltimore, MD 21203, and ask for your free *I Love Animals and Broccoli Coloring Book.*

🐾 Ask for a subscription to *Vegetarian Times* magazine for your birthday. The monthly magazine is packed with recipes, interviews with celebrities who are vegetarians, and the latest info on how you are affected by what you eat. Find out more at www.vegetariantimes.com, or write to P.O. Box 420235, Palm Coast, FL 32142-0235 for a 12-issue subscription. Another magazine you might like to try is *Veg News,* which comes from California. You can check it out at www.vegnews.com, or by calling 415-665-NEWS.

🐾 If you just can't get enough information on vegetarian living, all the yummy vegetarian foods, and, most importantly, the animals, you mustn't miss PETA's www.petakids.com Web site, where you will find everything from facts, recipes, stickers, celebrities, and ideas for activism to a whole bunch of related links. You can also order your free Vegetarian Starter Kit and comics called *A Cow's Life* and *A Chicken's Life.*

🐾 If you love computer games, try Steer Madness (available at www.PETAmall.com), where you get to play a bull who luckily escapes a slaughterhouse and sets about saving other animal friends through a series of exciting missions.

🐾 Contact the Vegetarian Society at www.vegsoc.org and request *Going Veggie: A Guide for Life,* an activity pack for young people (aged 11–15 or 16–19) by filling in a request form on the Web site.

CHAPTER 4

Be Science Fair

Which do you think rats prefer?

> a. Maize (Indian corn)
> b. Mazes

The answer, of course, is a. Sadly, lots of rats end up in mazes because of old-fashioned science lessons!

Did You Know?

Some pretty grisly and senseless experiments still show up at school science fairs. For example:

🐾 Students have forced rats to inhale cigarette smoke even though everyone knows by now that smoking is hazardous to human health!

- A student in Pennsylvania deprived mice of vitamins as a science fair project. Many became frantic and hurt each other. Some even ate their babies, probably out of panic.
- A high school student in California actually cut out a frog's brain and timed how long the frog could swim around before dying.
- In New York, a student strapped a mouse into a homemade rocket, not thinking about how scared the mouse would be or worrying about injuring or killing him when the rocket lost power and fell back to earth.
- Other students use computer programs, not mice, for their science fair projects. David Liu made a computer model showing how the human brain and eyes work together so we can understand what we see. He won first place in the California State Science Fair and received $40,000!

You can study nature respectfully. Here are just a few of the things you can learn about without harming *anyone*:

- Without bats, we might not have bananas. Busy bats pollinate banana trees. Read up on bats to find out more.
- Ants have been seen "holding hands" to make a bridge so that others can cross a stream. Study ants by watching a neighborhood ant hill—from a distance.

THEY DID IT!

Three thirteen-year-old students, Kathlyn McMasters, Rachel Cosner, and Samantha Piazza of Abington Heights Middle School in Pennsylvania, compared vegetarian and meat-based diets for their school science project. The girls' science teacher said their project, which showed that vegetarians are less likely to develop cancer, heart disease, obesity, and other ills, "was, by far, the best one on display."

🐾 Deer only have twins if there's lots of food, and they have no fawns at all if there's a severe food shortage. Read books about how deer control their own populations, no thanks to hunters!

For lots of book titles to look up, go to Chapter 38, "Be a Bookworm."

What You Can Do

We don't need to dissect frogs or force rats to breathe cigarette smoke to understand what their insides look like or to learn that cigarettes are harmful. There are far more creative ways to enter the science fair:

🐾 You can make colorful charts that show how the human body works. Study diagrams on-line, or in encyclopedias and biology textbooks to learn about parts of the body and how they work together.

🐾 If you'd like to study animals for your science fair project, travel to *their* homes and observe their natural behaviors without interfering. Record birdsong and analyze it for patterns, see if you can figure out how many kinds of edible berries wildlife depend on or how a beaver makes her home, which is called a sett.

🐾 Swap the project where you are supposed to feed rats sugary sweets for one where you count calories and carbohydrates in what *you* eat. You'll learn a lot more!

🐾 Do a science project on animal rights or the environment, on why results from animal tests often don't apply to humans (quite often) because our bodies are different, on high-tech alternatives to animal tests like high-speed computer programs, or on elephants' incredible memories and the way they talk at low levels to each other over miles and miles of ground.

🐾 The Animal Welfare Institute suggests observing the squirrels in your neighborhood. If you pay close attention to their behavior and appearance, it won't be long before you are able to identify each one. Note how they chase and play with each other, how they react to birds and other animals, and the time of day they are most active—but resist the urge to interfere with and tame them.

Check It Out

🐾 Study humans. For example, chart the blood pressure of your classmates. For other projects that help you study yourself, ask your science teacher to call or write to Intellitools for information on their computer programs Physiogrip and Flex-icomp. They can be contacted at www.intellitools.com, by phone at 1-800-899-6687 or e-mail info@intellitools.com. You can also write to Intellitools at 1720 Corporate Circle, Petaluma, CA 94954.

🐾 You can contact the Animal Welfare Institute at www.awionline .org and browse through all their on-line publications, e-mail awi@awionline.org, or write to P.O. Box 3650, Washington, DC 20027. They have a neat little guide called *The Endangered Species Handbook*. It is full of ideas on how you can study animals without hurting them and is available on-line at www.endangeredspecieshandbook.org.

CHAPTER 5

Chicken Out

I stopped eating chickens
When I was only eight
I'd rather Henny had a life
Than lie here on my plate!
—Gabrielle Martin, age thirteen

"As far as chickens go, there are a lot of horrendous things
that go on behind closed doors . . . be it keeping them in tiny
quarters packed together, or sawing off their beaks, just the
atrocities that happen. People should be aware of it at least,
and know how cute those little chicks could be."
—Alexander Greenwald, Phantom Planet

Did You Know?

- Butterscotch, a little hen in Woodstock, Illinois, loved people so much that she would run down the farm's dirt road to meet visitors. Then she would hop up and down at their feet until they picked her up and cuddled her in their arms.

- Lucie, a rooster (in spite of his girl's name), lives with a family in Great Neck, New York. Lucie stands on a chair at the dinner table with them and eats from a plate. He's always checking to see if people have something on their plate that he doesn't have. He loves to be with people. If they raise their voices, he chimes in so loudly that it's impossible to shout over him, and everyone winds up laughing.

- Gonzo, a rooster, was given to children as an Easter gift. When he grew up nobody wanted him, so someone fed him poison. When that didn't kill him, someone wrung his neck and put him in a garbage can, where he almost froze to death. A garbage man rescued him and gave him to a kind person. For a long time Gonzo could only give raspy gurgles, but after six months Gonzo finally crowed again, and in his good new home he lived to a very old age.

- Hens and their chicks talk to each other even while the chicks are still inside their eggshells! Hens make at least eleven

different peeps and clucks to talk to their chicks for as much as two days before the chicks hatch.

- Chickens can memorize and recognize up to 100 other chickens and have up to 30 different "clucks" to say different things!
- Why did the chicken stop in the middle of the road? To lay it on the line! Today, hundreds of millions of chickens never get outside—they live inside dark, smelly egg factories. They spend their whole lives jammed into cages so small they can't even stretch a wing. Their bodies get sores on them as they try to turn around. When they lay an egg, it rolls away on a conveyor belt.
- The billions (yes, billions!) of chickens raised on factory farms each year in the United States never meet their parents, let alone get a chance to be raised by their hen mothers. They will never take dust baths, feel the sun on their backs, breathe fresh air, roost in trees, or build nests.
- In the time it takes you to read this page, approximately 5,000 chickens will have been killed in the United States for buckets, boxes, and dinner plates. Because billions of chickens are raised in huge, dirty factories, eating chicken causes millions of cases of stomach "flu" each year. Turkeys, geese, and ducks are also interesting individuals and are better as friends than as holiday centerpieces! They, too, suffer because people who never get to learn about them or know them think of them as dumb and unimportant.

What You Can Do

- Learn to appreciate chickens and other birds for the wonderful individuals they are. Tell people that each has his or her own special personality and feelings.
- When you hear other people refer to chickens, turkeys, or ducks in a mean or thoughtless way, tell them that these de-

lightful animals deserve kindness. Tell them all about Butterscotch, Lucie, Gonzo, and any other chickens you may know about. Find out more on the Amazing Animals section of www.goveg.com. You can help change people's attitudes.

🐾 Let others know that baby chicks belong with their mothers; they aren't toys to be given as Easter gifts. Write a letter to your local newspaper two weeks or so before Easter, telling readers why it's not cool to give chicks as gifts. Your letter can be as simple as this:

> *Dear Editor,*
>
> *I am [insert your age] years old and live in [insert your city], and I think that it's wrong to give or sell chicks for Easter. They are fragile and innocent and most people don't know how to take care of them. Some people are very cruel to them. Let them stay with their moms.*
>
> *Sincerely,*
> *[Your name]*

🐾 Stay away from any clothes or items with real feathers. Usually chickens or other animals had to die to provide them. If you have a feather pillow or comforter, buy a non-feather one when it wears out.

🐾 Try interesting, delicious, nutritious vegetarian foods in place of chicken, turkey, geese, ducks, and eggs. If you still like the taste of chicken, you can buy non-animal substitutes that taste almost the same and are much better for you. Yummy "fake chicken" nuggets and patties are made by Boca, and most big grocery stores sell them—ask your mom or dad to add them to the shopping list. For more ideas, check out all the other fabulous fake "meats" listed in Appendix B, "Tasty Vegan Foods to Try."

Check It Out

- Visit www.goveg.com. In the video section there are videos showing chickens learning from TV, navigating obstacle courses, and more. In the Amazing Animals section, you'll find out why scientists say that chickens are smarter than cats or dogs! There are also book and video recommendations, and more.
- Check your library for more true stories about chickens and other wonderful birds. Read about the sad ways millions of chickens and turkeys are raised for meat and eggs today.
- Check out the Don't Be a Chicken Chump Web site at www.petakids.com/chumps.html, order your free comic, *A Chicken's Life*, and remind your friends what KFC really stands for: Killing Friendly Chickens!
- For information about the factory farming of chickens, and for tips on helping put an end to it, write to FAWN (Farm Animal Welfare Network), www.fawn.me.uk/, or P.O. Box 40, Holmfirth HD9 3YY, UK.

CHAPTER 6

Save the Whales

Question: What do blue whales and rabbits have in common?

Answer: The blue whale's heart is the same size as a rabbit—a Volkswagen Rabbit! The blue whale is the largest animal ever to live on this planet—even bigger than any of the dinosaurs!

Question: Why are white whales also called canaries?

Answer: Because they talk to each other so often they've been nicknamed sea canaries for all the noisy chatter they make. White whales (beluga whales) would always be getting told "Shhhhush" if *they* were in your class!

Did You Know?

🐾 Whales communicate with sounds that carry very far underwater. When the ocean is quiet, a whale in Antarctica can hear the call of a whale in Alaska but, because of all the ships and boats on the ocean today, very often whales can't hear each other over long distances anymore. The noise from the motors of our ships must be awful to the whales' sensitive hearing.

🐾 When whales talk to each other it sounds like pings, clicks, and long musical notes to us. The communication between whales is so beautiful that people have recorded it and listen to it as they do other music.

🐾 Whales swim by moving their tail fins (flukes) up and down. The flukes of humpback whales are as different as people's fingerprints. Sometimes whales bang their flukes on the surface of the water just for fun.

🐾 Whales are mammals and need to breathe air. The blowholes on top of their heads are like our nostrils.

🐾 We call baby whales calves. Whale calves' aunts often babysit them when their mothers have to go somewhere.

🐾 Keiko, the real orca who starred in *Free Willy*, was released from captivity in 2002, just like the whale in the movie. Although, sadly, his stressful youth as a show-biz whale meant that Keiko died at 26 when wild orcas can live until they are 50 years old or so, his last years were spent enjoying the freedom of the ocean and companionship of his fishy friends and family.

🐾 Blue whales can weigh up to 150 tons (that's heavier than ten school buses), and they can eat one *ton* of food every day. Whales use their flippers for more than just swimming. One mother whale was seen slapping her baby with her flipper to teach him to stay away from a ship.

🐾 Blue whales, along with many other kinds of whales, are following the dinosaurs into the pages of history. They are becoming extinct because people have been killing them and selling their body parts. Whale meat is considered a "delicacy" in Japan and some other countries. The oil from their bodies has been used to make lipstick, shoe polish, margarine, and car transmission oil and is sometimes used to grease weapons. People kill whales with tusks (like the narwhal, who has a horn like a unicorn!) for the same reason they kill elephants: ivory equals money.

🐾 It is now against the law to kill whales for food anywhere in the world, but Japan and Norway are avoiding this law by claiming that they are killing whales to study them. The whales' meat is then sold in stores. People in other places have also been caught killing whales even though it's illegal.

> **Question:** Why do orca whales have so many fishy friends?
> **Answer:** An orca's only enemy is humans; they have no other natural predators.
> **Question:** Why do blue whales wish they had scales like some other ocean animals?
> **Answer:** Because blue whale babies can gain as much as 200 pounds in one day!

What You Can Do

🐾 Don't buy or accept anything made of ivory. If you receive a gift of ivory, thank the giver for the thought but ask them to return the item to the store—and explain why.

🐾 Although it is illegal to put whale oils in products in the United States, some cosmetics and some food may be imported from countries where it isn't. Always be sure to check lipstick, margarine, and shoe polish for ingredients like "marine oil," which can come from whales.

🐾 Protest any balloon launches at school fairs and other community events. Balloons can drift into the ocean, where whales and other and sea animals mistake them for food. The balloons get stuck in the animals' insides and can kill them. A boy named Chris Palmer wrote a letter to his school principal when he heard about a planned balloon launch. After reading his letter about all the dangers balloons pose to animals in the sea, the principal canceled the launch, and students planted colorful flowers instead.

A class of fourth-graders in Connecticut went to their

legislators and lobbied for a law to ban balloon launches in that state, and guess what happened? It is now against the law to have balloon launches in Connecticut!

🐾 Avoid going to aquariums and theme parks that keep whales and other sea animals in tanks, which, compared to their natural homes, are the size of bathtubs. (See Chapter 26, "Born Free, Bored Stiff.")

🐾 Get your class to join you in writing letters to the Japanese Embassy, 2520 Massachusetts Ave. NW, Washington, DC 20008, to ask that Japan leave the whales alone. Let the embassy know that you want whales to be around forever.

Question: Why are an orca whale's mother and father
    dolphins?
Answer: All orca whales are actually a kind of
    dolphin! They are the largest dolphin in the ocean.
Question: What part of a white whale might you also
    find in a fruit salad?
Answer: White whales have a flexible forehead area
    called a melon! They have flexible lips, too,
    meaning they can "pull faces" just like you.

Check It Out

🐾 Write to the Cousteau Society for more information about whales. You or your group or family can subscribe to the group's bimonthly newsletter, *Dolphin Log*, written especially for young people, by writing to the Cousteau Society, 710 Settlers Landing Rd., Hampton, VA 23669, or calling 1-800-441-4395, or e-mailing cousteau@cousteausociety .org. Check out their site especially for kids at www .cousteaukids.org.

🐾 Write to the Sea Shepherd Society for more information about whales and how you can help them. You can find them at www.seashepherd.org, P.O. Box 2616, Friday Harbor, WA 98250, or by e-mailing info@seashepherd.org or calling 1-800-4WHALES. If you join the group, you receive the *Sea Shepherd Log,* a newsletter describing how the group sinks illegal whaling ships (while no one is on them, of course) to prevent people from killing whales, and sails to Newfoundland to paint seal babies, which doesn't harm them but makes their fur worthless to people who want to kill them for their coats.

CHAPTER
7

Be Good to Bugs

Hurt no living thing:
Ladybird, nor butterfly,
Nor moth with dusty wing,
Nor cricket chirping cheerily,
Nor grasshopper so light of leap,
Nor dancing gnat, nor beetle fat,
Nor harmless worms that creep.

—Christina Rossetti

Did You Know?

🐾 Snails eat plants with their raspy tongues. They extend their two pairs of feelers by turning them inside out. The longer pair of feelers has eyes at the tips. In dry weather, snails seal themselves into their shells. They can live this way for four years!

🐾 An earthworm has ten hearts.

- Ants live in colonies and are very social. They have highly developed senses of smell and touch. They communicate with their antennae. Ants can lift 50 times their own weight and leave signals for other ants, telling them which way to go and not to go.
- Sowbug and pill bug babies emerge from their mother's pouch and ride for a few days under their mother's tail.
- Nobel Prize winner and famous humanitarian Dr. Albert Schweitzer, who tended the sick in the hospital he built in Africa, would always stop to move a worm from the hot pavement to cool dirt.

How Do You Rate?

Try out your knowledge of creepy crawlies with our true-or-false challenge:

True or False?

1. Crickets can hear using their legs.

2. A dragonfly can fly at speeds up to 36 mph.

3. Spiders always hatch exactly 100 babies.

4. The silkworm moth has eleven brains.

5. Snails move to a larger shell if they get too big.

6. Centipedes sometimes use small twigs to attack other insects.

7. Honeybees have hair on their eyes.

8. Ants carry small leaves as an umbrella in wet weather.

9. A cockroach can live more than a week with its head cut off.

10. Slugs have more sensitive hearing than dogs.

Answers—Don't Peek!: 1. True; 2. True; 3. False; 4. True; 5. False; 6. False; 7. True; 8. False; 9. True; 10. False

What You Can Do

Take time to look closely at small creatures. Sometimes you might try using a magnifying glass or binoculars. Be very careful not to scare, touch, or move these creatures. Imagine yourself in an insect's place:

🐾 You're standing on a leaf the size of a living room rug and then the wind turns your leaf over.

🐾 You're a moth emerging from a cramped, dark cocoon into a sunlit garden.

🐾 You, like many butterflies, moths, and other insects, have only a very few days of life.

How good it would feel if you were trying to get out of a house through a closed window and someone finally caught you carefully with a drinking glass and a piece of cardboard and released you outside!

Learn how fascinating insects are. Read books and ask your parents, teacher, and librarian questions about them. Keep a log of your observations. Leave insects alone; each has a place in the environment. Help insects if you get a chance. Remember, you can't save them all, but every once in a while a special chance to help one comes along.

- Prop a twig or two in birdbaths so insects who would otherwise drown can climb out. Check the twigs every so often to make sure they're still in place.
- If your porch-light fixture has an open bottom, as many do, cover it with a square of aluminum foil held on by a rubber band, so flying bugs won't burn to death on the lightbulb.
- If you come upon any injured bugs, give them a merciful death by stepping on them hard and quickly. This is kinder than letting them suffer helplessly.
- Help insects inside your home get outside to their homes. Never throw an insect into the toilet. One woman threw an ant into her toilet and came back later in the day to find him still swimming. She felt terrible, so she rescued him and put him in the yard.

Respect the rights of small water creatures in and along the banks of ponds, lakes, lagoons, rivers, and oceans to live their short lives without being handled or moved from their homes by people. In their *Endangered Species Handbook*, the Animal Welfare Institute recommends taking "a field trip to a flower" to observe insects at work.

- Start your studies before the plants bloom or when you first notice some of the flowers. Make a record of the way insects behave in the patch.
- Observe at different times of day, from early growth to full flower to the end of the growing season. Do not disturb the patch in any way that would alter the insects' environment.

- Tell anyone who teases you an interesting fact about bugs, so they will start to appreciate them more.
- Make a mini–nature reserve in your garden so that it is a comfortable place where small animals and insects would like to live. Here are some simple ideas:
  - Plant a berry bush for birds, butterflies, and insects to feed from
  - Buy a birdbath or make one from an old pie pan—make sure the water is less than two inches deep though, or small animals might fall in and get stuck.
  - Place some dead wood or an old tree stump in your yard— more than 150 species of birds, animals, and insects can live in one log!

Check It Out

- Borrow books from your library about insects and small water creatures. Then see if you can see any of the creatures in the book in your own yard.
- Join the Bug Club (www.projects.ex.ac.uk/bugclub), an on-line club and information page for kids who love creepy crawlies— or visit the All About Snails page (www.kiddyhouse.com/ Snails/snail.html) for great facts and fun activities on these intriguing creatures.
- Read the cute storybook *Diary of a Worm* by Doreen Cronin (published by Joanna Cotler, 2003), which gives a day-to-day account of life as the smallest son in a big, big worm family. And, if you like that, there's also *Diary of a Spider* by the same author!

(Much of this chapter's Did You Know information was provided courtesy of the Marin Humane Society and the Peninsula Humane Society Education Department.)

CHAPTER 8

Fur Is Un-fur-givable

Over 40 million other-than-human beings are killed every year just because of what they're wearing: fur! Human beings get their "secondhand" fur coats by killing tiny chinchillas, rabbits, beavers, fluffy baby seals, beautiful big cats like lynxes, and lots of other animals. Up to 15 beavers, 25 foxes, 35 raccoons, 40 minks, or 50 muskrats are killed to make just one fur coat!

Did You Know?

🐾 When the steel-jaw trap snaps closed on animals' legs, often breaking them, animals, especially mother animals, may chew off their own paws to get home to their families, and often they die of hunger or thirst or from struggling or be-cause they bleed so badly. Luckily, the steel leg trap has been banned in more than 70 countries as well as in Rhode Island, New Jersey, and Florida.

🐾 Other fur-bearing animals live on "ranches." But if that gives you the idea that the animals are lounging around on pillows, forget it! Almost always the animals are in cages, sometimes out in the snow, and never get a chance to feel the ground or play.

🐾 Lots of famous people refuse to wear fur, including top stars like Daniella Allonso, P!nk, Charlize Theron, Gisele Bund-chen, Sarah Jessica Parker, Brad Pitt, Jennifer Aniston, and Ben Affleck.

🐾 Fur once turned heads, but now it's turning stomachs! Dozens of stores don't sell fur anymore, including Sears, Kmart, Gap, J.Crew, Banana Republic, and Forever 21. Fashion designers like Stella McCartney, Betsey Johnson, Emanuel Ungaro, and Moschino won't put fur on their dresses and coats. Fashion magazines *Mademoiselle, In Fashion,* and *Model* refuse to run fur advertisements, and some of the largest fur companies have gone out of business.

🐾 Gentle beavers were once close to extinction because of a de-mand for beaver hats and collars. Beavers help humans by helping to stop erosion by very skillfully building "lodges" on rivers, layering mud and tree branches with their paws and teeth. People trap beavers for fur in underwater traps set outside the "lodges" where they raise their young and shelter them during the winter. Beavers drown in the traps.

🐾 Some of the animals killed for their pelts in China are do-mestic dogs and cats. Their heads are knocked on the pave-ment, then they are skinned and strangled with wire nooses so that their fur can be turned into collars and trim, toys, glove linings, and cat toys. Of course, these animals are no different than our own beloved companions. When PETA visited an animal market in southern China, they found animals in cages who still had their collars on! Approximately two million dogs and cats are killed for their fur every single year.

In 2004, PETA asked young people to take action against the fashion store Forever 21 by writing to ask that the store stop selling clothing made of fur and by not buying their products. More than 100,000 kids responded by writing letters— no wonder Forever 21 contacted PETA straight away! The company agreed to remove all fur from its stores and promised never to sell it again. Then, early in 2005, Forever 21 purchased competitor Gadzooks, and made its fur-free policy cover all 150 Gadzooks stores in 36 states, too!

THEY SAID IT!

Here's what some celebrities have to say about the cruelty of fur:

"Most people, if they knew how fur was made, if they knew how animals were killed, most people wouldn't be down with it. If you saw a guy hurting a puppy on the street, you definitely would say something, I know I would."

　　—Benji Madden, Good Charlotte

"I can look anyone in the eye and say that I think wearing fur is the dumbest thing in the world!"

　　—Chuck Comeau, Simple Plan

"I don't know why you would want to wear a dead carcass on your body!"

　　—Paul Brainerd, Silverstein

What You Can Do

🐾 Avoid anything at all made from animals' skins, including teddy bears made of mink and toys like "jumping spiders" made of rabbit fur or boots and scarves with furry pom-poms. Ask for coats made with materials that don't harm animals, like fiberfill or Thinsulate. These are even warmer than fur and have been worn in Antarctic expeditions and by climbers on icy Mount Everest.

🐾 Write to PETA (501 Front St., Norfolk, VA 23510) for free cards that explain why animals need their coats. When you see people wearing fur coats, hand them a card that says "We'd like you to meet someone who used to wear fur" and has a picture of a beautiful raccoon or fox on it. In department stores, you can put cards in fur coat pockets so someone else gets a lesson.

🐾 If you see furs being bought, sold, or given away in contests, speak up! Please complain in person to the store manager, write letters, get together with friends, or go it alone, and make phone calls, or even hold a local demonstration. When a group of students heard that fur was going to be displayed at a reception at their school in Fairfield County, Connecticut, 400 students signed a petition against the display. Guess what happened next? The display was canceled!

🐾 If you or a family member has a fur coat, consider giving it as a donation to an animal rights group like PETA (your parents will be happy to hear that it is a "tax-deductible donation"). It can be used in displays to teach others exactly how fur coats are made. Or check with a local wildlife refuge to see if they'll use furs for orphaned wild animal babies to snuggle with.

Check It Out

🐾 For more information on how you can combat the cruel steel-jaw leg hold trap, contact the Animal Welfare Institute at www.awionline.org, e-mail awi@awionline.org, or write to P.O. Box 3650, Washington, DC 20027.

Log on to the Peta Kids homepage (www.petakids.com/clothing_fur.html) and read all about how animals are hurt to produce fur. They also have lots of free information, stickers, and posters you can request, and contests to enter!

CHAPTER 9

Don't Pass the Product Tests

Testing on animals is immoral and cruel—
An animal should never be used as a tool.
So help cruel companies realize
Animals have their own interests and lives,
And cruelty-free products are the best buys!

—Gina Samsock, age twelve

"I think any testing for beauty products is so unnecessary.
There are so many successful companies selling good products
without animal testing. . . . I don't believe that you need
animal testing, like the ghastly eye test they do on rabbits—
they should know what to put in these things by now!"

—*American Idol* judge Simon Cowell (He
might be cruel to contestants, but he's
certainly no enemy to the animals!)

Until recently, many people thought "animal tests" meant shampooing rabbits' fur or putting cleansing cream on their whiskers. Of course, it means nothing of the sort. Every year, approximately

14 million animals (more than 38,000 animals every day) are used to test cosmetics, toiletries such as toothpaste and shampoo, and household detergents and other cleaners.

One of the ugliest and, sadly, most common tests on animals is called the Draize test. This is the one that Simon Cowell calls "ghastly"! For this test, liquids, gels, and powders are put into rabbits' eyes, and technicians write down how the eyes react. Some animals' eyes swell, and some animals even go blind. Acute toxicity tests are even uglier. Often called "lethal dose" tests, they measure the amount of a product it takes to kill part of a group of animals forced to swallow or breathe it.

Despite animal tests, people still get sick from swallowing products, getting them in their eyes, or spilling them on their skin. Testing products on animals seems even scarier when you think about how different our bodies are from a guinea pig's or a rabbit's. Animals used in product tests clearly feel pain, just as we do, but their bodies almost always react in a different way to drugs and other products. For example, aspirin helps most human headaches go away, but it kills cats, and penicillin kills guinea pigs but can help fight infection in humans.

There are many modern, humane, and more accurate ways to make sure the products we use are safe. With encouragement from those of us who refuse to buy products tested on animals, more and more companies are using test tubes, speedy computer programs,

human volunteers, weird and wonderful artificial human skin, and other methods that don't hurt animals.

Did You Know?

🐾 Animal tests for makeup and household use are not required by law, and they don't protect us. For example, dogs' skin and rabbits' eyes are very different from ours.

🐾 Companies that don't test on animals use human volunteers, human skin cells grown in laboratories, and other great methods, as well as known safe and natural ingredients.

🐾 Tobacco companies still conduct cruel tests using hundreds of thousands of animals even though we already know that smoking causes cancer, emphysema, and other health problems. Just another reason to never start smoking!

🐾 People around the world are working to make tests on animals illegal. The two tests mentioned above are already against the law in parts of Australia and Italy. Let's keep going!

🐾 Hundreds of companies do not test products on animals, including Hello Kitty, Strawberry Shortcake, Powerpuff Girls, Bonne Bell, Hard Candy, That's So Raven, Urban Decay, Revlon, Clinique, Avon, Bath and Body Works, The Body Shop, Stuff by Hilary Duff, and Method laundry products.

🐾 Cruel companies that won't stop testing on animals include Ralph Lauren, Cover Girl, Max Factor, Olay, and Clairol, as well as big companies like Coty who make products for Adidas, Calvin Klein, Davidoff, Glow, The Healing Garden, JOOP!, Kenneth Cole, Lancaster, Marc Jacobs, and Rimmel.

What You Can Do

🐾 Use only cruelty-free products. It's easy! Brittany Murphy, the star of movies like *Just Married* and *Love and Other Disasters*, says she is a sucker for the yummy cruelty-free Dr Pepper–

flavored Lipsmackers gloss by Bonne Bell. Fellow actress Alicia Silverstone (*Scooby Doo 2*, *Beauty Shop*, *Stormbreaker*) can't get enough of cruelty-free cosmetics either. You can follow their lead. Just take a look:

Inside Alicia's Cruelty-Free Beauty Bag:

Shampoo and conditioner: Kiss My Face, Lamas
Hairstyling: Prawduct
Toothpaste: Jason
Deodorant: Kiss My Face
Facial Cleanser: Boscia, Zia
For breakouts: Boscia
Eye makeup remover: Kiss My Face
Toner: Jurlique
Mask: Boscia, John Masters
Lip liner: Ecco Bella
Mascara: Gabriel
Eyeshadow: Zuzu
Eyeliner: Zuzu
Foundation: Kiss My Face
Powder: Ecco Bella, Zuzu
Blush: Ecco Bella

Moisturizer: Jurlique, Zia, Eminence
Concealer: Ecco Bella

Next time you're at the store, check out Alicia's beauty picks!

🐾 Write to PETA, 501 Front St., Norfolk, VA 23510, or log on to www.caringconsumer.com for free lists of hundreds of cruelty-free companies, and be sure to share them with your friends.

🐾 Read up on animal testing at the PETA Kids page (www .petakids.com/testing2.html) and download the list of bad companies who do cruel tests—take it with you when you go shopping and make sure you never buy those brands. Look out for PETA's Caring Consumer Product Logo. Anything with this label is definitely not tested on animals.

🐾 If you have animal-tested products in your bathroom or kitchen cabinets, ask if you can mail them back to the companies that made them (try sending the package COD, meaning the company pays the postage). Tell the companies you disagree with animal tests and find their product "unsatisfactory." Some companies may send you a refund. Here's a sample letter to the president of Procter & Gamble:

Dear President,

I am returning this bottle of Febreze because I find it unsatisfactory now that I know your company uses animal tests. Until you stop testing on animals, my family has decided not to buy any more Procter & Gamble products. Instead, we will buy cruelty-free cleaning products from companies like Method and Seventh Generation. Please send me a full refund, and please stop testing on animals.

Very disappointed,
[your name]

🐾 Be a positive nuisance! James Sexton, a teenager from New York, spent a day handing out leaflets in front of a store that sold perfume that had been tested on animals. By six that evening, the manager had pulled the perfume from the shelves.

🐾 Ezra L. Nolan Middle School's Critterpals invited speakers to talk to their classes about animal tests, checked out the school's supply closet for animal-tested brands, and persuaded the principal to switch to only cruelty-free supplies. The Critterpals topped off their five-month-long project by giving hundreds of dollars raised in their "penny drive" to their local humane society's rescued-animal sanctuary.

Check It Out

🐾 Visit www.caringconsumer.com and order a Cruelty Free Pocket Shopping Guide and find out which products are safe to buy.

🐾 If you have a PlayStation, tackle the PlayStation 2 game Whiplash (you can order it at www.petamall.com) and help a gang of groovy animals escape from Genron, a high-tech lab where innocent animals are used to test human products.

10

Horsing Around

One kid said to another, "I went riding this morning."
"Horseback?" asked his friend.
"Yup, he got back before I did."

In some places in the United States, such as Nevada and New Mexico, if you are lucky you can still see herds of wild horses running free across the land, kicking up dirt, flirting, eating all sorts of different kinds of grasses and shrubs, playing, and raising their families.

Wild horses are being pushed off the land they need to survive because cattle ranchers want to take away the wild horses' right to eat wild grasses. The ranchers would rather use the grass to fatten up their cattle so they can sell hamburgers, so they have convinced the government to round up many of the horses and sell them at auctions.

More than 200,000 wild horses have been removed from public land since 1971. Already six U.S. states have lost their entire wild horse populations! Lots of these poor horses end up being killed to make canned dog food.

On an island called Assateague, off the coast of Virginia, to raise money for the local fire station, wild ponies are chased across a river in the middle of summer every year, and their foals are sold to anyone with a wad of cash in hand. Many of the ponies aren't yet old enough to live without their mothers, and the people who buy them often don't know how much it will cost or what to do exactly to properly take care of a growing pony.

Did You Know?

- In Australia, friends are called cobbers. A cob is a small horse, usually a stout and solid one.
- Horses are closely related to zebras.
- Wild horses live in groups called harems made up of several females and one stallion. Harems are very close-knit family groups.
- Can you understand "horse"? Horses communicate by whinnying, neighing, making other sounds with different tones and patterns, and by moving their ears. Horses nuzzle and rub their heads on people and horses they trust. When certain Eskimos meet they rub noses, but when horses greet each other they sometimes put their noses together and blow into each other's nostrils!
- Horses in love stay close to each other. When they are afraid or think they may have to fight, horses rear up on their hind legs. They put their ears back flat when they are upset, and their eyes tell a million stories about the way they feel.

Like us, animals all over the world have lots of different rules to live by—but here are some hugely humorous horsy laws! Bet you didn't know that:

- In New York City, it is illegal to open or close an umbrella in the presence of a horse.

- Horses are required to wear hats in hot weather in Rosario, Argentina.
- In Wolf Point, Montana, no horse shall be allowed in public "without its owner wearing a halter."
- In South Carolina, no horses are allowed into Fountain Inn unless they are wearing pants.
- In Hartsville, Illinois, you can be arrested for riding an "ugly" horse.
- In Marshalltown, Iowa, it is against the law for a horse to eat a fire hydrant. (Well, that's a lucky law for the horse, unless it accidentally ate some chili!)

What You Can Do

- Write to your congressperson (United States House of Representatives, Washington, DC 20510) asking that no more money he given to the Bureau of Land Management for wild horse roundups (if you don't know the name of your congressperson, ask your librarian or do a quick search on the Internet). Tell your representative that you don't want ranchers kicking wild horses and other animals out of their home ranges. Explain that the land where the horses are being rounded up is public property belonging to all of us, and that the lives of horses are more important than eating hamburgers.
- People are trying to get the horrible roundups stopped. You can help by writing a letter of protest to the Refuge Manager, P.O. Box 62, Chincoteague Island, VA 23336, or e-mail FW5RW_CNWR@fws.gov. Your letter might look something like this one:

> Dear Refuge Manager,
>
> I just learned about the wild pony roundup. I am writing to ask you to stop catching these frightened

ponies and auctioning them off to whoever comes along. I love horses, but would never buy one who was taken away from her mother and sold against her will.

I am also upset about how the ponies are forced to swim across the channel from Assateague Island. I think this is very mean and must hurt and scare them.

I know the fire department needs to raise money to keep going, but there are a lot of other ways to do it. The horses should be allowed their freedom. Please stop the roundup and auction, and please don't write back and tell me it's okay, because it isn't.

Sincerely,
[your name]

🐾 Take up a collection for Black Beauty Ranch in Murchison, Texas, where wild horses find safety. The ranch has adopted many wild horses after they were rounded up unfairly by the Bureau of Land Management, and the horses now roam freely on more than 600 natural acres! Black Beauty Ranch has become a sanctuary for all kinds of animals.

🐾 When Melissa Sanders visited the "kiddie rides" at the town fair and saw ponies forced to walk in circles for hours in the hot sun, she was upset. But when she saw that the ponies were so skinny that their saddles didn't fit properly, she was angry. After she left the fair, Melissa wrote a letter to the fair organizers, the mayor of her town, and the editors of her local newspapers. She says, "People can't just do whatever they want to animals so that they can make money. I won't let them get away with being mean to the ponies again."

🐾 Help stop horse-and-buggy rides, which aren't as fun and romantic as they look. Tell people about how these horses have to pound the pavement all day long in the summer heat, pulling buggies full of people through traffic. If carriage-horse rides are offered in your town, write a letter of protest to the mayor or call the mayor's office. (Go to your local library for the mayor's name and address.)

🐾 Avoid riding stables. Imagine wanting to be out running in a sunny field, but you have a different stranger on your back every hour of the day, some people yanking on the reins, pulling on the bit in your mouth, and kicking you in the ribs. Hey, no way!

🐾 Bring carrots and apples to horses kept in stalls and fields. They love getting delicious treats to break up the boring day. Check the condition of the horses, too—are their hooves cracked, overgrown, and dry, or shiny and trimmed? Are their coats dull and dry or shiny and soft? Are the horses nice and round or skinny? If they seem sick or neglected, do the horses a favor and ask the local humane society to come and check on them.

🐾 Stay far away from horse races. When horses are injured or their feet hurt, people sometimes give them drugs to numb the pain—but make them keep racing. This makes their injuries even worse. Try to get your school to put on a "race against horse racing." Have three-legged races, sack races, and/or human wheelbarrow races, and invite the whole town to come and watch or join in. Ask for a donation at the door and send the money you collect to your favorite horse protection group. That way all the horses win!

Check It Out

🐾 For more information about the animals saved by the Black Beauty Ranch, visit www.fundforanimals.org/ranch/ or you can write to them at 200 West Fifty-seventh St., New York, NY 10019.

🐾 Write for information or join the Hooved Animal Humane Society (HAHS). It rescues abused and neglected horses and makes them well again by letting them live in a sanctuary until they can be adopted into good homes. You can find out more at www.hahs.org, by e-mailing to info@hahs.org, or by writing to HAHS, 10804 McConnell Rd., Woodstock, IL 60098. The Indiana Hooved Animal Humane Society (www.ihahs.org, or 6400 S. 650 W., Columbus, IN 47201) does many of the same things.

CHAPTER 11

It's Raining
Cats and Dogs

Anybody Have a Calculator?

Question: If 6 cats have 6 kittens every 6 months, and
each of those kittens has 6 kittens every 6 months,
how many cats would you have after 6 years?
Answer: 2,176,772,336! That's equal to more than a
third of the world's human population!

The number of homeless animals is more than we can imagine:
20 million dogs and cats who end up in animal shelters every year
in the United States never find a home. Yet pet-shop suppliers and
other people keep breeding even more cats and dogs—that's like
putting gasoline on a fire that's already out of control!

Did You Know?

🐾 Three to five thousand puppies and kittens are born every hour in the United States.

🐾 For every person who comes into the world, 15 dogs and 45 cats are born.

🐾 Animal shelters and pounds take in 27 million lost or abandoned dogs and cats every year.

What You Can Do

🐾 Have female cats and dogs spayed and males neutered so they won't have puppies or kittens. Both operations are quite simple and very safe. They also prevent some health problems and make animals less likely to wander off in search of a mate. Dogs and cats should be spayed or neutered as soon as possible—under six months of age—so that they won't add to the overpopulation problem. Every litter hurts because every home you find for the new puppies or kittens is a home taken away from an animal sitting in a shelter, waiting for someone to love them.

🐾 Say pooh to pet stores! If you or your family are looking for a dog or cat to adore, contact your local animal refuge to find out who is up for adoption. Many of the animals sold in pet stores come from puppy "farms" where female dogs are kept outdoors in pens. Their puppies are taken from them, packed into crates, and shipped, sometimes hundreds of miles, to the mall—when there are already enough abandoned animals in shelters who need a loving home like yours!

Check It Out

- Chances are, your local animal shelter has leaflets you can hand out to encourage spaying and neutering. If not, write for free flyers to PETA, 501 Front St., Norfolk, VA 23510, or visit www.helpinganimals.com for more information and to order PETA's Spay/Neuter information brochure.
- Read the book *One in a Million* by Nicholas Reid (Raincoast, 1997). It tells the story of Joey, a young stray dog who finds himself away from family at the local animal shelter and follows his quest for a loving home. You can find it on-line at www.petabookstore.com, or ask your local library to order it for you.

CHAPTER 12

"Companimals"*
Are Priceless

"I was raised by a mother who always had great compassion and respect for animals. It was instilled in me. I grew up that way. So when I see dogs or other animals suffer, it's just been something close to my heart."

—Charlize Theron (from a speech made at
PETA's Humanitarian Awards gala)

---

*"Companimals" is short for "companion animals" —a more loving and respectful term for the animals many people call "pets."

How much is that doggie in the window?" Don't ask! If you and your family decide to bring an animal into your home, adopt one (or two) from a shelter. That way you can save a homeless animal, and your money won't be used to support the dog and cat population explosion.

The goal of pet shops is to make money, so animals in them are often treated as just another "item" to be sold. This means many of them are not well cared for: they go without the love, care, and attention they need to grow up healthy in body and spirit.

Did You Know?

- "Puppy mills" in the Midwest supply pet shops with most of their dogs. In these places, mother dogs and their litters usually live in small, outdoor cages, with wire mesh bottoms that make walking uncomfortable. Because of their difficult start, puppy mill pups can grow up a bit crazy, maybe easy to scare or angry, or with bones that aren't as strong as they should be. "Purebred" dogs are not better than "mutts," because they *are* mutts: they are mixtures of other dogs bred by people who wanted dogs with short noses, long legs, or barrel chests, for example. Hands off! Mutts don't have as many problems as purebreds do and are no less special.

- To get certain looks for hunting, fighting, or showing off, some people still cut ("crop") the ears of dogs like Dobermans and cut off ("dock") dogs' tails.

- Greyhounds have been used by humans for hunting and "sport" since the days of the ancient Egyptians. Greyhound racing is still big business today, even though it is illegal in 34 states. These poor pooches just never get a break! Many die or are destroyed when they suffer broken legs, heatstroke, or heart attacks. Others—such as Randad, a dog in Alabama— are victims of the machinery used to make them run fast on the race track. Randad jumped onto the lure rail and was electrocuted.

❀ Happy II, a retired Greyhound who was abandoned in the hot Florida sun, is one of the lucky ones! Rescued by a passerby, he was rushed to the hospital by the National Greyhound Foundation and spent six weeks fighting for his life. Today he lives in a loving home with his best friend, a big white turkey named Tom, three other Greyhound pals, a cat, and lots of other dog buddies.

❀ The animals sold at pet stores may look pretty, but the story behind them isn't! For every "exotic" bird (that is, one who comes from another country) you see in the store, four or more others are likely to have died during their capture or transport to the United States. They, and other exotic animals like lizards and snakes, usually don't live very long when they get to the U.S., because they come from tropical forests or deserts where the climate and the food supply are very different.

❀ Some pet shops also sell animals who aren't exotic but who still want to be free, like turtles, fishes, prairie dogs, and ferrets. More and more breeders are trying to sell different animals such as mini-pigs and llamas as if they were trendy toys. Once in people's homes, these animals can easily suffer because most people don't know exactly how to care for and feed them, although the pet-shop people don't talk about that.

What You Can Do

❀ Purchase leashes, toys, and other supplies for companion animals at supply stores that don't sell animals.

❀ Animals belong in their natural habitats, so never buy a caged bird, exotic animal, or companion animal. Protest the sale of animals like these with complaints, letters, or a demonstration (or all three).

❀ The Animal Welfare Institute suggests that you:

- Visit pet stores in your area and make lists of the wild animals being sold. If you find an endangered bird, reptile, or other animal, immediately contact the nearest office of the U.S. Fish and Wildlife Service to report it. The USFW's number is in the phone book. There is a list of endangered species in the Animal Welfare Institute's *Endangered Species Handbook.*

- Check the store for cleanliness and see whether you think the animals are healthy. If the cages are dirty or if the animals have dull coats or seem just plain tired, call your local humane society right away.

- The Animal Welfare Institute would also like to hear about your investigation. Go to www.awionline.org and e-mail awi@awionline.org, or write to P.O. Box 3650, Washington, DC 20027 for information on exotic animal trades.

❀ Say "no thanks" to tanks. Avoid tropical or other fishes. Like birds, fishes are interesting animals and accustomed to living in big groups and having a lot of space in which to move about.

❀ You can help to educate Greyhound racing supporters by leafleting at a local track. Even if your state has a ban, it probably has breeding kennels that are supplying dogs to other states who haven't, like Alabama, Arizona, Arkansas, Colorado, Connecticut, Florida, Iowa, Kansas, Massachusetts, New Hampshire, Oregon, Rhode Island, Texas, West Virginia, and Wisconsin. You can find a leaflet called *Greyhound Racing: The Real Losers* to download or order at www.petaliterature.com.

❀ Write letters to the editors of your local newspapers explaining why it's important that we put an end to the cruel "sport." You can find fact sheets and more information to help with your letter at www.peta.org or by calling PETA at 757-622-PETA. Check out Chapter 25, "Write On!" for tips on letter writing.

THEY DID IT!

Fifth- and sixth-graders in the Animal Club at Radcliffe Elementary School in New Jersey convinced their local mayor to create and pass a Care of Animals law. Thanks to this, dogs can't be kept outside for more than eight hours a day and they have to be given warm dog houses with straw, food, and clean water. Violators of the law will be fined up to $5,000 or serve 90 days in jail—as well as facing a very angry bunch of compassionate kids!

🐾 When you are ready to adopt an animal, seek out dogs or cats who may not seem "cute" to other people. Old, weird-looking, and even scruffy animals need love just as much as any others—maybe more.

Check It Out

🐾 If you or your friends are looking for a new animal companion, forget the pet shop and adopt an abandoned animal who *really* needs a home. Your first stop should always be your local pound or animal shelter. Wagging tails and purrs await!

🐾 Another place to take a look is www.petfinder.com, where you can post a classifieds ad, find out about the animals at your local shelters—or sign up to be a volunteer dog walker or cat cuddler!

🐾 Actor and PETA pal Charlize Theron stars in a video asking people not to buy puppies from pet stores but to adopt companion animals from animal shelters. The video is available on loan from PETA at www.peta.org.

🐾 Write to PETA, 501 Front St., Norfolk, VA 23510 for a fact sheet on what other things to look out for in your local pet store.

❀ There are more than 200 greyhound rescue groups in the U.S., the U.K., and Western Europe who save the dogs and give them loving homes. For more information visit the Web sites of the Greyhound Protection League (www.greyhounds .org), which organizes adoption programs throughout the U.S. and distributes information about the racing industry, and the National Greyhound Foundation (www.4greyhounds .org), and GREY2K USA (www.grey2kusa.org), who are lobbying for legislation to put a stop to greyhound racing.

❀ If you want more ideas on the kind of things to look out for, visit www.helpinganimals.com. You'll find lots of information there on how you can become a real angel to the animals.

CHAPTER 13

Pen Pals for Animals

Question: What did the envelope say to the mail carrier?

Answer: Stamp out animal cruelty!

Did You Know?

🐾 People all over the country—and all over the world—care about animals: from Athens, Georgia, to Athens, Greece; from Paris, Texas, to Paris, France; and from Venice, California, to Venice, Italy. Everyone, no matter what language they speak, understands what being kind means.

🐾 Some animal protection groups can put you in touch with new friends both close to home and far, far away.

🐾 You can learn a lot from your pen pal. You'll be able to swap stories and ideas, even share recipes.

🐾 Overseas pen pals can keep you updated on animal protection in their countries, and you'll be able to help by writing letters on behalf of animals in other countries.

🐾 When one vegetarian family in Australia started writing to a vegetarian family in England (who'd placed a pen pal ad in a magazine) they had no idea what a lasting friendship it would become. More than 20 years later, the two families are still writing and have even traveled across the world three times to visit each other and cook up big cruelty-free feasts together!

What You Can Do

Write a letter about yourself:

🐾 Do you live with any other-than-human beings? Tell about them—their names, their ages, how you met them, what they're like, and how you look out for them.

🐾 Do you have any hobbies? Do you play sports? Do you collect anything?

🐾 What kind of music do you like to listen to? What kinds of books do you like to read?

🐾 Do you like to paint or draw?

🐾 Describe the area where you live.

Check It Out

Send your letter to one of the groups listed below:

🐾 Contact the Animal Aid Youth Group at the Old Chapel, Bradford Street, Tonbridge, Kent TN9 1AW, UK, e-mail youth@ animalaid.org.uk, or visit the site www.animalaid.org.uk/ youth, where you can find out how to exchange letters with other people your age who are interested in animal rights.

🐾 The Veg Source Web site has a special spot where you can place an ad for a vegetarian and animal caring pen pal or reply to other people's posts. This is for people of all ages, but there are often a lot of kids looking for pals listed. Check it out at www.vegsource.com/talk/penpal.

- Log on to www.studentsoftheworld.info, an international pen pals site where you can list your interests and find a suitable pal. The site has connection to e-mail buddies and regular mail as well as links, games, and blog options.

- The Vegetarian Society runs a service to connect veggie pen pals under 17 years old through their Web site www.vegsoc .org/community/penpals.html, or write to the Vegetarian Society, Parkdale, Dunham Rd., Altrincham, Cheshire WA14 4QG, UK for more information.

- VIVA! (Vegetarians International Voice for Animals) runs Youth Write to Reply, a groovy snail-mail and e-mail service for vegetarian and vegan kids looking for pen pals. Visit www.timetogoveggie.com/youth, write to VIVA! 8 York Court, Wilder Street, Bristol BS2 8QH, UK, or e-mail info@viva .org.uk to register.

- Much of the African wildlife is endangered or threatened with extinction and many young people of Africa are committed to saving it. They would like to share the information on these animals with you. To be put in touch with a pen pal in Africa, visit www.wildlifeclubsofkenya.org, e-mail info@ wildlifeclubsofkenya.org, or write P.O. Box 20184, 00200 Nairobi, Kenya. They also have a kids' magazine, *Komba*, which you can read on-line.

CHAPTER 14

Watch Out for Animals

When Abraham Lincoln made his driver stop so he could put a baby bird back in her nest his friends made fun of him, but he told them, "I could not have slept tonight if I had left that little creature to perish on the ground." What a great man! He knew how very important it is to always be on the lookout for animals in your environment and make sure they receive any help and care they may need.

Did You Know?

🐾 Each August, children on the Icelandic island of Vestmannaeyjar conduct nighttime rescue operations to save pufflings (migrating baby puffins) who fall to the ground after mistaking the city's lights for the moon. The puffling rescue is very important to the children, who release the birds on the beach the next morning. Staying out late to find the pufflings is "a lot better than Halloween," says rescuer Arny Osvaldsdottir.

🐾 A ship's crew usually keeps four-hour watches, but two-hour watches are called "dog watches."

🐾 Squirrels have a built-in "air-conditioning" system! They sit still with their tails arched over their backs and covering their bodies to help keep warm in the winter and cool in the summer.

THEY SAID IT!

Here's a fab story from the band Goldfinger about saving animals while on tour:

"I was just getting some food when I saw a tank of about 30 lobsters and they were all just petrified . . . so we were saying a prayer for these animals, for these souls. They were going to be boiled the next day, and I said, 'This isn't enough. I've got to do something.' So I just took out my credit card, and I just bought all the lobsters because it was so brutal. Even the people at the food market, they don't see these animals as alive. They're just putting them in paper bags on top of each other . . . they just couldn't understand why I was going to buy these animals to let them go. They said, 'Don't you understand that there's just going to be more in here?' But one life is enough, just one life. Take one life and give it a chance to live. . . . So we just went to the edge of the pier, and let these animals back into the ocean, and maybe half of them lived, maybe one of them lived—but they were guaranteed to die, guaranteed to be boiled alive if I'd left them there."

—John Feldmann, Goldfinger

What You Can Do

Even if your neighborhood isn't full of pufflings to rescue, there are still lots of animal friends who need your help, like squirrels, birds, and cats and dogs:

🐾 Set up a neighborhood meeting for kids who care about animals.

🐾 Post notices of the meeting at your neighborhood school, supermarkets, and libraries.

🐾 Go door to door with flyers. (Your newspaper carrier might help.)

🐾 Choose a name for your group. You could even have a special password, hand sign, or animal call.

🐾 At the meeting, have everyone think of past animal emergencies. What went right and what went wrong? Write down all the helpful tips and make a list of problems to solve.

🐾 Educate your community about animals! Make a poster of your list, including pictures of all the kinds of animals living in your community, and put a copy of it on every neighborhood door.

🐾 Make a list of numbers to call for help when animals are lost, found, hurt, or being mistreated or when they need new homes, and give it to everyone in your neighborhood (your local humane society can probably give you these numbers). Your list should look something like this:

Kindness Club Neighborhood Animal Watch

1. SMITH COUNTY HUMANE SOCIETY: 111 Walton Road; 555-2224. Lost dogs and cats (only) picked up; Mon.–Fri., 3–5 P.M. Will take in animals Mon.–Sat. until 9 P.M. Has low-cost spay/neuter program.
2. SMITH COUNTY POLICE DEPT: after-hours pickup of injured animals; 555-6084.

3. DR. JONES, EMERGENCY VET: 555-2471 until 5 P.M., 555-7082 after 5 P.M.
4. BIRDS: Jenny Adams, 555-4119 or 555-4045*** or Gary Fisher, 359-0088.
5. WILDLIFE: Mark Johnson (all), 555-9996**** or Trudy Marshall (squirrels only), 555-9075.
6. OTHER ADULTS who will help when needed:

Carol Anderson, 555-2256*
John Brown, 555-1239**
James Thompson, 555-4455*
Marcia Malone, 555-9976*****
Kim Talbot, 555-6789*

Add more names as you get them. Make sure they are people who really care.

*Has holding place for dog
**Has holding place for cat
***Has holding place for bird
****Has holding place for wild creature
*****Has holding place during weekdays

Here's what to do if you find an injured animal:

- Someone should stay with an injured animal while someone else calls for professional help.
- Be careful! A dog, cat, or wild animal can bite from fear when hurt. Don't touch them or get close if you don't need to, and when you do lift them, be slow and gentle and use heavy gloves and a blanket.
- You can calm wild animals by placing a large cardboard box over them (punch air holes in the box first).
- Baby birds who are just learning to fly are often out practicing with their mothers in the spring. Leave baby birds alone. Their mothers are almost always nearby or getting food for

them. If you find a baby bird who is injured, or is still alone after dusk, put him or her gently into a little box with air holes punched in it and call a wildlife rehabilitator, a person licensed to take care of injured and orphaned wild creatures. Wild animals who trust people could get themselves into trouble later if strangers try to harm them, so the rehabilitator helps them learn to get along again on their own and, when they're healthy, releases them in a protected area. To find out if there's a wildlife rehabilitator in your area, call your local humane society, park district, or a veterinarian.

🐾 Injured dogs or cats may feel better if someone puts a blanket over them (leave their heads out!) and talks softly.

🐾 If an animal needs to be moved, be very gentle. Depending upon the animal and the injury, you might use a board, a heavy jacket, a blanket, or a car mat. Try to get an adult to help.

She Did It!

When she was nine years old, Dakota Goodall from Idaho learned from the PETA Web site (www.petakids.com) that animals need exercise. So she decided to ask busy neighbors if she could walk their dogs for them. She didn't ask for any money; all she wanted was for the dogs to be running around and getting fresh air. That was just the start! Dakota also goes to her local animal shelter and donates blankets, toys, and snacks for the animals and hands out flyers during the summertime around her neighborhood, letting people know that dogs should never be left in hot cars because it's dangerous. Dakota's motto is: Happy Animals Make a Happy World! "I love animals," she says, "and I hope that people who use them for clothing and food realize that they are not helping our world in any way."

🐾 If the animal is in the road, be sure you get an adult to help. Run to a nearby house and/or flag down a motorist. Do not risk your own safety by standing in the road.

🐾 Take inspiration from Dakota and distribute seasonal "alert" flyers that remind people about proper animal care. Tell your community:

- That dogs need to live indoors with their human family but some people keep their dogs outside alone in the cold and these dogs need good, solid doghouses to help protect them from the weather.
- That straw is far better than blankets in doghouses during winter (blankets can get wet and freeze up).
- Not to leave animals in a car on a hot day.
- How they can control fleas, by flea-combing and vacuuming frequently, as well as adding brewer's yeast and garlic to their companion animal's food.

🐾 Adopt a "shut-in"! Is there a lonely dog living in a backyard in your neighborhood? All dogs need love and companionship. Neighborhood "watchdogs" like Dakota can try getting permission to walk lonely dogs and to sit or play with them. Once you start, don't break their hearts by not coming back (see Chapter 1, "Do Unto Others," for dogs' needs).

   Do the dogs have doghouses that protect them from the weather?

They should be:

- Up against the humans' house, not out in the middle of nowhere
- Made of wood
- Set off the ground a few inches, facing south
- In a shady spot in summer
- Filled with straw
- Warmed by having a door flap (a car floor mat, slit with a blade in several places, works well) nailed on to keep out wind, rain, and snow

🐾 Make sure:
- The dogs have fresh water in a clean, tip-proof bucket, and that the water's not frozen in the winter.
- They are being fed properly.
- They are not ill (if they seem sad or weak, are bleeding anywhere, have a cough, or otherwise seem sick, call for help).
- The chain or rope (if they're tied up) can't get tangled around things like bushes, trees, chairs, and the like. In many places, tying and chaining is not allowed by law.
- Their collars aren't cutting into their necks (remember, three of your fingers should fit under the collar).

🐾 And, finally, are the dogs spayed or neutered? The last thing a forgotten dog needs is a whole family of forgotten dogs!

If any of these things needs attention, politely ask the dog's guardian to fix them, or fix them yourself, with permission. If they won't and you can't, call your local humane society for help.

Here's what to do if you find stray animals who need help:

🐾 Put them in a safe place until their real home can be found. If you can, bring them into your house, and give them a little food, water, attention, and something to sit on. If you can't take care of them, ask a friend to, or check your Neighborhood Animal Watch list to see who can. As a last resort, take them to a good, clean, and humane local shelter, and check up on them often until you find their real guardian—or a good new one.

🐾 Call in a "found" report to your animal shelters and local newspapers. Many newspapers will run a free "found" ad. Since someone could pretend to be an animal's guardian and then sell him or her to a laboratory for experiments, don't give out details about the animal in the ad. Instead, have the person who calls do all the describing.

🐾 When animals need new homes, be careful! They are counting on you to find a home where they will be loved and cared for forever. Hang on to the animal if you have doubts about the person who says they will take him or her. Wait for another home you *know* will be loving.

🐾 Make sure the dog or cat gets "fixed" (spayed or neutered) before the adoption, or, if the animal is too sick, be sure the new guardian signs an agreement that it will be done very soon. Sample agreements are available from PETA.

🐾 If you run out of time, it is kinder to take animals to a well-run shelter than to give them to not-so-good homes.

Check It Out

🐾 For loads of information and free downloadable fact sheets on what you can do to help companion animals and wildlife in your neighborhood, visit www.petakids.com, www.peta.org, and www.helpingwildlife.com, or write to PETA (501 Front St., Norfolk, VA 23510) and ask them to send you out Companion Animal and Wildlife fact sheets.

🐾 Go to www.helpinganimals.com and read up on how to find a responsible shelter and the guidelines for finding a good new home. You can also order a Placement Pack, which will help you with information on finding the right home for a companion animal.

🐾 Learn how to save a lobster like John Feldmann did! Log on to www.peta.org for a downloadable fact sheet on saving lobsters and check out the *Being Boiled Hurts* leaflet at www.petaliterature.com.

CHAPTER 15

Dump Wasteful Habits

How Do You Rate?

Take this quick quiz to find out how much of an environmental expert you are:

1. You have a picnic on the grass in a park with friends. At the end of the day you have lots of empty soda cans. You:
   a. Decide to play a game by throwing them in the lake to see whose can goes the farthest.
   b. Tie them up in a plastic bag, find the nearest trash can, and tip them all in.
   c. Look for a recycling bin but when you can't find one, decide to take the cans home to recycle—you know that if you leave them in the park they'll literally take *200 years* to break down!

2. You're out doing the grocery shopping with your mom and you end up with the biggest cart of things you've ever seen! At the checkout, you:
   a. Ask for all the items to be placed in separate plastic bags so you can carry them to the car easily.
   b. Ask for as many items as possible to be put in each plastic bag so you don't end up with too many bags to throw away when you unpack them.
   c. Pack all the groceries in the big cloth reusable bags you've brought from home and suggest to the store manager that the store start supplying cloth or paper bags.

3. You and your friends are playing on the beach and you see a pile of plastic bags on the sand. You:
   a. Are happy because you were just looking for a place to leave your trash.
   b. Don't think it's a nice to see trash on the beach and decide to go to a different beach next time.
   c. Get your friends to help you clean up all the plastic bags and take them to a closed trash can where they won't blow back on to the sand, then look around to see if there's anything else that needs to be cleaned up along the sand.

4. Your dad's just finished mowing the lawn and asks you to help clean up all the clippings. So you:
   a. Rake them all into a bag and carry them to the trash.
   b. Leave them where they are—they'll decompose eventually.
   c. Gather up all the clippings and use them to start a compost pile to turn all your family's food and garden scraps into nutritious soil for the garden.

Mostly a's Uh-oh, an Earth slob? You seriously need to brush up your skills in helping the planet! Finding out more about the way your actions can help or hurt the environment could help you to change how you behave. Check out the groups listed at the end of this chapter for tips and ideas.

Mostly b's You know what's right and what's wrong when it comes to caring for the environment, but you don't always do what you know to be the right thing. Work a little harder at putting your knowledge into action. Check out the environmental groups listed at the end of this chapter for ideas on how you can become more earth friendly.

Mostly c's You're an Earthling of the best kind! A true champion for planet Earth, you know exactly what to do for the environment—and you always do it. You're also not afraid to teach your friends and family how they can be less wasteful too. Keep it up!

Did You Know?

🐾 One Thanksgiving, Mary Beth Sweetland saw a duck whose beak was caught in a plastic six-pack holder. The six-pack holder made it impossible for him to eat. Mary Beth had to work hard to win his trust. Every day for two weeks she coaxed him ashore with soothing words and cracked corn. Finally, "Mr. Quackster" came close enough for Mary Beth and a friend to snip the plastic ring, freeing the duck from litter that would have taken his life. As he flew away, Mary Beth says all she could do was sit on the bank and smile with joy.

🐾 A dead sea turtle was found with enough plastic garbage in her stomach to carpet the floor of a large room. Turtles can mistake plastic for food and die when it clogs their stomachs.

🐾 Littering is costly to all of us. Picking up litter and getting rid of it in our nation's parks costs $15 million a year—enough to buy a Nintendo game for every single person in Tucson, Arizona.

What You Can Do

It causes problems at home when we make a mess. When we mess up the whole planet, the problems multiply and affect millions of plants and animals!

Imagine how you'd feel if you stepped on broken glass with bare feet (you might have done this accidentally—it hurts!) or got your nose stuck in the opening of a soda can.

🐾 Why not organize a litter pickup? Get your family, friends, and neighbors to help you. Each person should carry a sturdy bag for collecting cans, bottles (be careful of broken glass), papers, and gum and candy wrappers (are any yours?) along the road, in the woods, or around a pond. If you do it every fourth Saturday, you could pick a different site each month.

🐾 Organize litter patrols along creeks and streams, in meadows, and on the street. And, whether you're walking to school or tramping through the woods, keep an eye out for—and always pick up—cans, wrappers, six-pack rings, and so on. Give a small prize for the person who picks up the most or the most interesting or unusual trash!

🐾 Recycle all kinds of stuff! Start a recycling program at home and get everyone involved at school, too. Most recycling centers take newspapers, aluminum cans, and glass. Many take plastic and metal food cans as well. Look in the Yellow Pages under "Recycling Centers" for one near you.

🐾 Before throwing away or recycling plastic six-pack rings, snip each ring so that animals don't get their heads caught in them. Rinse out empty metal food containers really well and smash the open end closed so small animals can't get their heads caught in them.

🐾 Try to use everything over and over again before you throw it away. Bring plastic and paper grocery bags back to the store with you every time you shop. Use them until they fall apart! Better yet, buy or macramé a string mesh or canvas bag you can use all the time.

🐾 Have a yard sale. Sell your old things that you don't want anymore because, as they say, "one person's trash is another person's treasure!" What you can't sell give away.

🐾 Start a compost pile in your backyard for organic garbage, like food scraps, coffee grounds, and grass clippings. This kind of "garbage" turns back into dirt full of nutrients to feed the Earth. Luckily, one-quarter of all our garbage is organic waste!

Check It Out

🐾 For hundreds of household products that are safe for the environment (including reusable shopping bags!), check out the Seventh Generation on-line catalog at www.seventhgeneration .com. You can also find their products in some general stores and supermarkets.

🐾 Visit the Defenders of Wildlife site at www.defenders.org. Request some of their fact sheets on our endangered environment and register for free e-mail wildlife updates. You can also write to them at 1130 Seventeenth St., NW, Washington, DC 20036, call 1-800-989-8981, or e-mail defenders@mail .defenders.org.

🐾 The Earth Care Paper Company produces note paper, office paper, envelopes—anything papery you can think of—from all recycled materials. They can also send you information on recycling and composting your own household waste if you write to them at P.O. Box 7070, Madison, WI 53707, or phone 608-223-4000.

🐾 Write to your state's Division of Solid Waste. They should have lists of all the recycling programs and places in your area so you can ask your school cafeteria staff to use one. For a list of all kinds of recycling programs and activities, visit the Waste Prevention Information Exchange database at www.ciwmb.ca.gov/WPIE.

- Be a part of a beach cleanup or start one yourself. Visit www.beachcleanup.org or check out the Ocean Conservancy at www.oceanconservancy.org and e-mail, write, or call them for more information on their activities (The Ocean Conservancy, 2029 K St. NW, Washington, DC 20006, 1-800-519-1541).
- Write to the Environmental Defense Fund for ideas on how you can help keep garbage to a minimum. Visit them on-line at www.environmentaldefense.org, or call them at 1-800-684-3322.

Free the Fishes

We've all heard that fishes are smart because they live in schools. Well, some fishes are so smart that they've come up with truly clever ways to hide their babies when they sense danger.

Guess where mother cichlid fishes hide their babies:

- a. In a snorkel.
- b. On a boat.
- c. In their mouths.

Letter c is correct. Some fishes open wide and let their babies swim right inside their mouths if a big fish comes after them. Other fathers, such as cardinal fishes, actually carry the eggs that hold their babies in their mouths until they hatch!

Did You Know?

- 🐾 The first hitchhikers were fishes called "remoras," or "sucker-fishes." These fishes actually hitch rides with sharks and other large sea animals by attaching the sucking disk (sort of like the plastic suction cups you can put on windows) they have on top of their heads to the shark's head or tummy.

- 🐾 A French man named Alphonse Alais invented a frosted fish tank for shy fishes!

- 🐾 Fishes never close their eyes.

- 🐾 Fishes use their mouths for many things that people do with their hands: collecting food, building homes, and taking care of their babies. Because of this, their mouths are very sensitive, so fishes get badly hurt when caught on hooks. Even if the fishes are thrown back into the water, their lips are wounded and can become infected.

- 🐾 John Bryant, author of a lovely old book called *Fettered Kingdoms*, says that the three things needed for fishing are "a hook, a line, and a stinker!" By "stinker" he means the cruel people who think killing fish is fun.

- 🐾 Fishes can be very caring. A South African magazine reported a true story about a deformed goldfish named Blackie and his friend, Big Red. Blackie had trouble swimming, and for over

a year Big Red kept constant watch over his sick friend, gently carrying him on his back and swimming him around the tank. Every day, at feeding time, Big Red picked Blackie up and swam to the water surface, where they both ate together!

🐾 Some people think fishing is a relaxing way to spend a day, but it certainly isn't relaxing for the fishes! Most people don't realize that fishes do feel pain, like all living creatures.

🐾 Careless people often litter lakes and streams with fishing line. Egrets, ducks, fishes, muskrats, opossums, and other animals who come to the water for a drink get tangled and sometimes strangled in this sharp plastic string.

🐾 Goldfish do not have a three-second memory! In fact, they have been proved so far to have a memory of up to 11 months. Work done at Plymouth University and the National Marine Aquarium has shown that goldfish can learn a route through a maze. After a many-months-long break, they can be put back into the maze and still remember which way to swim. Other fish also have amazing memories; salmon always return to the river they were born in to spawn after years of growing up out in the oceans!

THEY SAID IT!

Here's what Andy Hurley, the drummer from Fall Out Boy, has to say about being friendly to fish:

"Being vegetarian means that you don't eat meat—fish is meat, and it's a living creature, and it's wrong to eat living creatures. I remember a story that a friend of mine once told me. He's a vegan and his parents are vegan. They called themselves 'vegetarians' but they ate fish until one day they caught a fish that mated for life—and the other fish swam around until it died because they'd caught its mate. They stopped eating fish and became vegan because of that."

HE DID IT!

After Glenview Springman Middle-Schooler Kevin Pratt saw how many fish died at his local Goldfish Day (where park officials dump 1,000 live goldfish into the pool for children to retrieve with nets and buckets and bring home as pets), he decided to challenge the tradition, pointing out that the fish suffer and die from exposure to chlorine and trauma. He collected 200 signatures on a petition that called upon the park district to substitute vinyl goldfish for the live ones. "Every animal, no matter how small, is due respect," Kevin said. "They're goldfish, but they're still creatures of this Earth," he told a reporter for the *Chicago Tribune*. "Whatever their purpose is, they should still be given a chance to live."

What You Can Do

- If someone asks you to go fishing, explain why you won't go. Tell them that fishes deserve to live just like anyone else. Suggest a game of Go Fish with cards or going bird or fish *watching* (but not disturbing) instead.
- If your school, carnival or fair has contests that give away free goldfishes as prizes, organize a group of students to complain to the principal. Explain that a frightened, lonely goldfish is no prize, and suggest plush animal toys or other neat non-living prizes instead.
- If you already have a fish tank, be super sure it's kept at the proper temperature (78° to 82° F for fresh water and 76° to 78° F for salt), is placed somewhere safe but where the fishes can look out, and has a rock garden and aquatic plants for fishes to hide in. In case the power goes off, make sure there is a battery as a backup.
- Spare the fishes whenever you can! If just looking a bit odd meant you didn't count, a whole lot of people I know would

be in deep trouble. And, anyway, because of water pollution, fish flesh can be full of mercury and other chemicals that cause human cancers, as well as other contaminated junk that isn't good for us.

Check It Out

🐾 Contact Pisces at www.pisces.demon.co.uk or write to Pisces (BM Fish, London, WC1N 3XX, UK) or e-mail them at pisces@pisces.demon.co.uk. They have lots of informative fact sheets on how you can help end sport fishing and also have special pages just for caring kids like you.

🐾 Write to PETA, 501 Front St., Norfolk, VA 23510, and visit PETA's site www.fishinghurts.com for lots of facts on fishing and ideas for action. If your dad likes to fish and you want him to stop, download the free comic *Your Daddy Kills Animals*, which will help you explain to him in a playful way why it is such a cruel sport and will help you argue your case if he still disagrees.

🐾 Read up on the list of veggie "meat" at the back of this book. You'll find loads of substitute "seafood" like Tuno and amazing "mock lobster" and "fake shrimp" from May Wah (www .vegieworld.com) who even makes abalone, crab, and more fishy fare—all from soy proteins!

VEGETARIANS SAVE **95 LIVES** A YEAR.

Art Impact

T. J. Schneider is a professional snowboarder, animal person, and artist too! He has been snowboarding since 1994—now, he's one of the biggest names in the sport. When he's not killing it on the slopes, he spends his free time playing his guitar, going to shows, and creating some awesome artwork. When PETA approached him to feature in an advertisement he asked if he could draw his own pictures for it. He says, "I like to draw birds, not eat them."

Drawing, painting, scribbling, and writing are all good fun and are great ways to get your message about helping animals out there. Take a tip from T.J. and get your whole class into the act!

Did You Know?

🐾 On a wall bordering Ocean Park Boulevard in Santa Monica, California, an artist named Robert Wyland has painted a beautiful mural of a mother gray whale with her calf alongside dolphins swimming free in a turquoise sea. It attracts everyone's attention as they drive, walk, or skate by. Your class could do a mural that would get just as much attention as this famous one!

🐾 If you can't get someone to let you use a wall, no worries! A mural on a piece of canvas is also a great way to call people's attention to animals.

🐾 A mural will last for years.

🐾 A wall mural could become a landmark.

🐾 A canvas mural can be displayed at school, at a fair, at a shopping center, at a bank, and in many other places.

You can get fancy if you like or keep it simple.

Here are some drawings to get you started. These were sent to PETA by caring kids who wanted to use their crayons for more than just the coloring book:

What You Can Do

🐾 Ask your art teacher, camp counselor, or club or group leader if your class can paint an animal mural. A mural could be painted on a school wall, in the cafeteria, on a concrete wall in the neighborhood, or in any suitable place in or outside of school. Construction companies sometimes welcome murals to brighten up their wooden walls at construction sites.

🐾 If scribbling with a ballpoint pen is more your style, take inspiration from comic book fanatics like Seth in *The O.C.* or Adam in *The Perfect Man* and draw your own comic strip. Design an animal rights superhero whose mission is to fight animal cruelty, and draw a strip of one of his or her winning battles. Make photocopies and share it with friends, or submit it next time you get a free topic art or writing project or to your school newsletter or magazine.

🐾 A canvas mural could be either one huge piece of canvas or many squares or rectangles of canvas that could be laced or sewn together later, or attached to one huge piece of canvas backing, to form the completed project. Have each class make one or several sections of the mural or canvas.

   Some theme suggestions are:

- A modern Garden of Eden, with people and animals living in harmony. (Don't forget the chickens, cows, pigs, and turkeys!)
- Companion animals being walked and played with by their guardians; add a message telling about the importance of protecting animals.
- An underwater scene at a coral reef or a partly underwater scene at the edge of a lake.
- A scene with forest animals, saying something like "The original owners of fur coats thank you for not wearing their skins."
- Animals leaving their circus cages and returning to the jungle, with a caption like "Animals belong in their natural homes."

Check It Out

- 🐾 Check with an art supply store about the materials you need. Select "environmentally friendly" materials when possible. Choose synthetic-hair brushes rather than mink or pig bristle brushes, for instance. Write to many different animal protection groups for a variety of information and pictures, from wolves to mice, to help you with ideas for your artwork. Check your school and public libraries for pictures and information, too.

- 🐾 Log on to www.petakids.com—PETA's on-line resource for kids, which is loaded with images and ideas for artwork—as well as free inspirational comics and regular design and drawing competitions you and your class can enter.

CHAPTER 18

Help Turtles Out of Trouble

Sea turtles live in the water, but sometimes they come up on the beach. Guess why sea turtles go to the beach:

a. To get a tan.
b. To lay eggs.
c. To build a sand castle.

Letter b is correct. Turtles use their back flippers to dig a hole, lay their eggs in the hole, and then cover them up again—all without looking!

Did You Know?

🐾 Sea turtles have been on the Earth for 100 million years and live to be more than 100 years old!

🐾 Sea turtles live in the water but breathe air. When sleeping, they can stay deep in the water for hours without going to the surface for air. When awake during the day, they have to swim to the top every few minutes to take a deep breath.

🐾 Sea turtles lay up to 100 eggs at a time. When the baby turtles hatch, they start running for the ocean as fast as they can. They know that the sea is there by the reflection of the moon shining on the water's surface. Like salmon and swallows, turtles return to the place they were born when they're ready to have babies of their own.

🐾 Other kinds of turtles live on land. Box turtles are the only ones who can completely disappear into their shells, which protect them from all other animals—except humans who want to eat them or use their shells to make eyeglass frames or ornaments.

🐾 Because we have built so many roads, box turtles find that they often have to cross streets to get to good nesting sites. In places where there are curbs, the turtles are too small to get over them and often end up falling over onto their backs. They get stuck that way until someone kind comes along and turns them the right way up. Some turtles keep walking along the curb looking for a low spot and get their feet burned from the hot pavement in the summer. Some cities like Minneiska, Minnesota, and Tybee Island, Georgia, have done a wonderful thing. They have put up warning signs for people in cars to be careful not to run over turtles who cross the street. Some neighborhoods on Long Island, New York, are thinking about lowering their curbs for the turtles. How nice!

🐾 The desert tortoise is in danger of becoming extinct. As you can probably guess, these tortoises live where there are very few trees but lots of low shrubs to eat and hide under. Ranchers, who often rent land from the government for their cattle to graze, are the problem. The cattle eat all the shrubs, roots and all, and leave the turtles nothing to eat and nowhere to sleep.

🐾 All-terrain vehicles (ATVs) and three- and four-wheel motorbikes also cause problems for tortoises and turtles. People may not see the little fellows and run them over by mistake, and their bike paths tear up the turtles' homes.

🐾 Snapping turtles have tails as long as their bodies. Like a person in a bad mood, they will chomp in your direction if you try to pick them up. They're not mean; they just worry that you are going to do them harm and they don't want to leave their spot.

Think you got what's totally true when it comes to turtles? Are you a top trainee in tortoise tidbits? Come out of your shell with a quick quiz and show what you really know. True or false?

1. The alligator snapping turtle wiggles a special worm-like part of its mouth to attract fish.

2. The longest-lived tortoise was over 500 years old.

3. Female Asian forest tortoises nest in trees to lay their eggs.

4. Some turtles can live for more than a year without food.

5. Some land turtles can actually out-run a human on level ground.

6. The male musk turtle produces a nice smell to attract females.

7. If box turtles eat too much they can get too big to fit inside their shells! Oh, my!

8. Only one out of 1,000 sea turtles survives after hatching.

Answers: 1. True; 2. False—but some have lived until 200!; 3. False; 4. True; 5. True; 6. False—in fact they release a terrible smell to scare predators!; 7. True; 8. True—sadly, many of the reasons for this are: humans stepping on the eggs, digging them up, putting up lights in the other direction so the turtles get confused and head to the highway, or getting in the way of the turtles' race to the sea.

What You Can Do

🐾 If you find turtles in a safe place, leave them alone or you'll give them "shell shock"! All turtles have things to do and places to go. If you find turtles in a place that isn't safe, like out on the roadway, gently carry them to the woods or a park nearby, and let them go. Turtles shouldn't ever be "pets." Like us, they want to live free, be with their friends, and have their own families.

🐾 If you already have a turtle (one that you or somebody else found, perhaps) at home or school, contact a local wildlife rehabilitator (ask your local shelter or humane society for names and phone numbers). Wildlife rehabilitators can help turtles who have been kept as companions get used to living free again.

🐾 If you or a friend have a turtle from a pet store or some other captive situation, or you know of turtles who need rescuing (perhaps in a school project), contact the New York Turtle and Tortoise Society at http://nytts.org/, or e-mail QandA@ nytts.org. You can also write them (NYTTS, P.O. Box 878, Orange, NJ) 07051-0878. They keep a list of rescuers who can help.

🐾 If you see turtles on their backs at the side of the road, carefully turn them over and put them well away from traffic. When moving turtles out of the road, be careful not to put yourself in danger (get an adult to help you) and not to put them in ditches or very rocky places. Look for nice flat areas of grass or dirt and put them down gently, facing in the same direction they were trying to go. Long-tailed turtles might be snapping turtles, so be *very* careful not to put your fingers anywhere near their mouths. They can be safely moved out of the street with a long-handled shovel—used gently, of course. Be gentle, too, when turning them back over onto their stomachs, and place them the right way up on a soft, grassy spot so you don't hurt them or crack their shells!

🐾 If you find injured or sick turtles (if, for example, their shells are cracked or they're bleeding), take them immediately to a turtle specialist. They have special glue they use to fix shells. Call your local humane society or zoo for the name of a turtle expert nearest you.

🐾 Add saving desert turtles to the long list of good reasons for not eating beef! The less beef we eat, the less risk there is of cattle ruining the turtles' homes and eating all the turtles' food. You can save turtles and cows at the same time.

🐾 Discourage people from using SUVs and four-wheel-drive cars and trucks in the desert. If they don't want to tear up their own backyards with those wheels, they should consider how unfair it is for them to tear up the homes of turtles, lizards, birds, and other interesting beings.

🐾 Shy away from real tortoiseshell brushes, ornaments, or jewelry; make sure it's plastic before buying anything that looks like tortoiseshell. And that goes for anything that might be made of an animal's horns, skin, shells, or hooves.

Check It Out

🐾 Write to the Sea Turtle Restoration Project for more information on helping these beautiful animals. Visit their site www.seaturtles.org, e-mail info@seaturtles.org, or write to Sea Turtle Restoration Project, P.O. Box 400, Forest Knolls, CA 94933. You can also call them at 415-488-0370.

CHAPTER 19

Stick It to 'Em!

Question: What did the lovesick animal rights sticker say to the handsome notebook binder?

Answer: I'm stuck on you!

Did You Know?

🐾 Skateboarding legend Ed Templeton is the designer of two popular models of vegan skate shoes for the shoe company Emerica. Get yourself some of the stickers he designed for PETA and deck out your board with the slammin' message I ONLY BUY AND WEAR NON-LEATHER SHOES FOR THE ANIMALS' SAKE! You can order your stickers by going to www.petacatalog .com or by calling PETA at 757-622-PETA.

🐾 With stickers you can add style to those boring notebook binders and at the same time tell your classmates and teachers that you are an animals' champ.

- You can use stickers or rubber stamps to educate mail carriers with every letter you send (read on to find out where you can get both).
- Brighten up your bike—really rockin' bikes are those that have animal rights stickers all over them!
- Bedazzle bumpers with animal stickers! Give your parents, brothers, sisters, and friends (hey, anyone who drives!) stickers to put on their car so they can use traffic time to tell others on the road that animals need to be protected.

- Put a button on your jacket, and then, even with your *lips* buttoned, you can still tell others it's not cool to be cruel.

What You Can Do

- Order stickers, leaflets, and cards about animal testing to have on hand for whenever you find a chance to tell someone what's up with it. Order as many free animal rights stickers as you like and use them to decorate your lockers and folders—that way you're spreading the message every time you're at school or in class. A good place to start is at the PETA on-line mall (www.petamall.com), where you'll find a heap of stickers, as well as iron-ons. You can also buy a ruler that has a list of 10 "rules" for being compassionate to animals on one side. That makes a neat gift!
- Order a custom-made rubber stamp with your own message from an office supply store or mail-order service. Use it to

decorate envelopes, letters, and just about anything with animal-friendly phrases like STOP ANIMAL TESTING or VEGETARIANS EAT FOR LIFE.

- Plaster animal rights stickers all over your notebook binders, folders, bike, skateboard, and (better ask first!) the family car.

- Call a sign shop and find out how much it would cost to have magnetic backing cut and applied to your bumper stickers. Every day you'll be able to move your stickers to different positions on your car—on the hood, the roof, and on the doors. At PETA mall you can also get a cool gift for your parents so that they can show off what a compassionate kid you are. Check out the bumper stickers with messages like PROUD PARENT OF A VEGETARIAN and PROUD PARENT OF A STUDENT WHO WON'T DISSECT.

- For your locker, glue magnets on the backs of stickers that still have backing, and you won't get in hot water because they won't stick permanently, or put up posters instead.

- You can order buttons from party supply stores with any animal message you want. Think of mottos, draw your own pictures, or clip photographs of animals out of magazines; or make your own if your group or club has a button maker. That way you can sell buttons to others at your school—or whenever you set up an information table and use the money to buy . . . even more stickers!

- Make sure that every restaurant menu you open that features meat gets an information card about the cruelty and dangers of eating animals, so that the next person who stops by for a burger learns the facts. Use PETA's Vegetarian Starter Kit business cards, a cute cartoon piggy brochure that lists information about the site www.goveg.com and tells people how to get a free Vegetarian Starter Kit. You can download or order these cards at www.petaliterature.com, by contacting PETA at 501 Front St., Norfolk, VA 23510, or by calling 757-622-PETA.

Check It Out

🐾 Stop in or call any local office supply store and ask about ordering a personalized hand stamp to decorate mail and other surfaces with messages. If you have trouble finding a local store, write to Metro Stamp and Seal Company, 9425 Georgia Ave., Silver Spring, MD 20910, or call 301-587-0151.

🐾 Most animal rights and animal welfare organizations have stickers for free that display messages against animal cruelty like RATS HAVE RIGHTS, MEAT IS MURDER, or FUR IS DEAD. A good place to start is the Humane Society of the United States (www.hsus.org) or the PETA mall on-line (www.petamall .com), where you can browse with your mouse for stickers—including the awesome design by Ed Templeton!

🐾 To start your own button-making business, order a starter kit (includes a hand press and other materials) from Badge-A-Minit. It can be purchased through their Web site www .badgeaminit.com or by calling 800-223-4103.

20

Call for Compassion

Can't get a ride to the circus protest? Let your fingers do the walking! Fur companies, cruel cosmetics companies, and others who hurt animals often have 800 or 866 phone numbers that you can call for free. These numbers let companies keep in touch with the people who buy their products (or, in your case, who don't buy them!), and you can call to let companies know that kindness to animals—not greed— is *your* priority and what you want them to do to change.

Did You Know?

🐾 800 and 866 numbers are paid for by the company that advertises them, not by you, so you can talk for as long as you like. In fact, the longer you talk, the better for the animals. When you have politely stated your opinion to the operator, ask to be transferred to a supervisor. If he or she hangs up, you can call back. Become a member of the "frequent phoner" club!

What You Can Do

🐾 Have a theme party! Next time you and all your friends are arranging a get-together at someone's house, why not suggest a "phone protest party." Everyone can take turns picking numbers from the list below and making your (and the animal friends'!) voices heard.

The following companies sell or promote fur. If you, your parents, or your friends are on their mailing list, you might want to say something like "Hi. I just got your catalog in the mail and couldn't believe that your company is still selling fur coats. Animals are killed for fur in awful ways, and they deserve their lives, just as we do. Please don't send me any more catalogs until your company stops supporting such cruelty."

🐾 Broadway: 1-800-626-4800 or e-mail concerns to@broadwayfashion.ca
🐾 Neiman-Marcus: 1-800-825-8000
🐾 Saks Fifth Avenue: 1-800-871-SAKS
🐾 Seattle Fur Exchange: 1-800-445-MINK, or go to www .seattlefur.com and fill in the on-line feedback form
🐾 USA FOXX & FURS: l-800-USA-FOXX, or e-mail to info@ usafoxx.com

The companies below still test their products on animals. Let them know you're a caring consumer and won't buy their products until they stop testing. Try something like "Hi. I just found out that your company tests its products on animals. There's no excuse for blinding and poisoning animals. Hundreds of companies don't hurt animals to test their products, so my family won't buy your products until you make the switch, too."

🐾 Arm & Hammer: 1-800-524-1328
🐾 Bristol-Myers: 1-800-468-7746
🐾 Clairol: 1-800-223-5800

🐾 Clorox: 1-800-292-2200
🐾 Colgate-Palmolive Co.: 1-800-221-4607
🐾 Elizabeth Arden: 1-800-326-7337
🐾 Johnson and Johnson: 1-800-526-3967
🐾 Kimberly-Clark Corp. (Kleenex): 1-800-544-1847
🐾 Nina Ricci: 1-800-245-6462
🐾 Procter & Gamble: 1-800-638-6204
🐾 Procter & Gamble (Cover Girl): 1-800-543-1745
🐾 Schering-Plough (Coppertone): 1-800-842-4090

Tell these two companies to say "Whoa" to the rodeo. For years, they've been major sponsors of this "sport," in which scared animals are prodded, roped and poked, and slammed to the ground, sometimes up to speeds of 25 miles per hour! You might say something like "I am upset to hear that your company still sponsors rodeos. Have you ever thought about how animals suffer in rodeos? Or how they are sent off to the slaughterhouse when they are injured or worn out? My friends and I will not buy your products until you stop supporting animal abuse."

🐾 Adolf Coors Company: 1-800-642-6116
🐾 Coca-Cola: 1-800-GET-COKE

Ever wonder why the government gives money to keep animal farms in business when eating meat can cause illness? Here's your chance to ask (and see if you believe the answer)! Call the USDA hotline (Mon.–Fri., 10 A.M.–4 P.M. eastern standard time) with your complaints and questions about the meat industry. You might ask, "Why does the U.S. government give so much money to flesh farmers when raising and killing animals for meat does so much harm to the earth, the animals, and me?"

🐾 USDA's Meat and Poultry Hotline: 1-800-535-4555

This company supplies schools and laboratories with animals for dissection and experiments:

🐾 Charles Rivers Laboratories: 1-800-LAB-RATS

The last two companies listed below are the country's two largest suppliers of animals for classroom dissection. A PETA investigation showed that many of the animals were mishandled and badly treated before they arrived on classroom lab tables. Call these two companies and Charles Rivers Laboratories and tell them something like "I don't believe rats and other animals are our tools to use and throw away as we like. I'm doing my best to make sure my school doesn't order anything (or anybody!) from your company. Why not sell only modern teaching tools?"

🐾 Carol Biological Supply Company (CBSC): 1-800-334-5551
🐾 Ward's Biology: 1-800-962-2660

Check It Out

🐾 Please note! Sometimes when companies begin to get lots of phone calls about their treatment of animals, they change their phone numbers. If this happens at any of the above companies, contact PETA (757-622-PETA) for information about how to reach them, or make a free call to an 800 operator at 1-800-555-1212 to ask for the new listing.

🐾 If you want to find out whether any other companies not mentioned here have 800 or 866 numbers, ask an 800 operator if there's a listing.

CHAPTER
21

Check Out the Entertainment

Did You Know?

🐾 Some circuses travel 12,000 miles every year. You would have to drive across the United States from San Francisco to Washington, D.C., four times even to come close to the number of miles many circus animals travel in 12 months! You know how boring long trips are, so you can just imagine how the animals must feel, cooped up in hot rail cars and in cages in trucks wondering where on earth they're going. No doubt this makes them sad and even angry, but many animals used in circuses, like tigers, bears, and alligators, have their teeth and claws removed so they can't strike back.

🐾 In 2005, an elephant named Gildah died all alone in a small exhibit cell at the Mirage Hotel in Las Vegas. Like most elephants in zoos and circuses, she was probably in lots of pain from the arthritis and foot disorders caused by her confinement in the hard concrete enclosure. She was the twenty-third elephant owned by Ringling Bros. and Barnum & Bailey Circus to die since 1992, including three tiny baby elephants.

🐾 People who go to the circus don't often think about how the animals behind the costumes and bright lights come to be there at all. If you see animals performing tricks, use the checklist in "What You Can Do" below to tick off the problems you see.

🐾 Animals in circuses learn their tricks by being prodded or beaten. Because they are afraid of being hit with a bull hook, a whip, or a shock prod, they know they must perform stupid, uncomfortable, and sometimes dangerous tricks. I mean, since when did you see an elephant in her homeland in Africa standing on her head? If you weighed a whopping four or five tons, you probably wouldn't want to do that either!

How Do You Rate?

Take a quick quiz to find out how much you know about what the animals in the circus *really* love to do:

1. One of a bear's favorite activities is to:
   a. Wear a tutu and perform dances.
   b. Pick and eat wild berries.
   c. Walk on tightropes.

2. Lions have very strong legs so that they can:
   a. Run quickly over long distances when hunting for food.

    b. Jump high enough to get through the circus hoop.

    c. Won't get tired walking from their enclosure to the big top.

3. A chimpanzee's favorite things to do include:
    a. Riding a bicycle.
    b. Making a nest out of soft leaves to sleep on.
    c. Wearing a colorful top hat and waistcoat.

4. An elephant's trunk is important because it:
    a. Helps her to balance on a ball.
    b. Gives the person riding the elephant something to hang on to.
    c. Can reach up into trees to collect leaves and fruit to eat.

Answers: 1. b; 2. a; 3. b; 4. c. Now you know that being trained to perform boring and dangerous tricks are none of these animals' favorite things!

What You Can Do

Go only to "animal-free" circuses with human performers. Avoid the circus if there are animals in it because the animals are not volunteers; they don't get paid and they don't ever get to leave. If you do see performing animals, use this checklist to record the problems you see:

- Are the animals wearing chains and muzzles? Are they wearing silly costumes that must be uncomfortable for them?
- Does the trainer hold a whip or a stick?
- Can you spot any sores, cuts, or scars on the animals?
- Are animals forced to jump through flaming hoops? (Animals are afraid of fire.)
- Do they look happy or sad?
- How many unnatural and dangerous stunts do the animals

perform, such as riding bicycles, skating, "dancing," walking upright, and balancing on a ball?

Send your checklist to the local paper with a letter asking others to stay away from animal circuses. Or ask your teacher to have a discussion group or let you write a paper about what you've seen.

❀ Imagine yourself in the animals' shoes (or roller skates!). Your class could think of something they don't like to do, like mowing the lawn or giving speeches in front of your class, then ask themselves: What if I had to do it twice a day, every single day of my life? How would I feel if I were kept in a small cage when I wasn't forced to do chores? What if I could never go outside to hang out with my friends or do anything fun? It's easy to understand why animal performers look so sad and lonely!

❀ When a circus comes to your town, write a letter to the editor of your local newspaper. Your letter will give many people a peek behind the scenes. Let people know that while many kids may dream of running away to the circus, animals must dream of running away *from* it. Your letter might look something like this:

> Dear Editors,
>
> Recent advertisements for the circus have bothered me very much. I told my parents I do not want to see the circus this year because now I know that circus animals have a very hard life. They spend many of their days traveling with little food or water in uncomfortable train cars. During training, they may be whipped or beaten. Bears have even had their noses broken. It makes me sad to see elephants standing on their heads or tigers jumping through rings of fire because I think they would rather be running through the jungle or

sleeping in the grass. My family and I will not be
going to the circus, and I would like others to
consider not going either.

Sincerely,
[your name]

🐾 Get a group together to protest outside the circus. You can
dress up as clowns (does anyone you know juggle or ride a
unicycle?) or wear animal costumes or masks and hand out
information. If you know people who can juggle or ride a
unicycle, bring them with you. Like the dog who went to the
flea circus and stole the show, you may too! Many people
aren't aware that animals may not be having a good time; let
them know better.

Check It Out

🐾 Round up your family and friends to see the Cirque du Soleil
(Circus of the Sun), the New Pickle Circus, or Cirque Éloize.
These are fabulous circuses that use only human performers
like fire eaters, trapeze artists, clowns, hula hoopers, jugglers,
and sword swallowers.

🐾 Visit PETA's Web sites www.circuses.com or www.petakids
.com/circus.html for fact sheets, on-line petitions, and protest
letters and to order your free comic, *An Elephant's Life*.

🐾 Pat Derby used to train tigers in the circus but she left the
spotlight and formed the Performing Animal Welfare Society
(PAWS), a group devoted to helping animals who are made
to work in circuses, films, and television. You can find out
more at www.pawsweb.org, by e-mailing info@pawsweb.org
or writing to Performing Animal Welfare Society, P.O. Box 849,
Galt, CA 95632.

🐾 Another group called PAWS is the Progressive Animal Welfare Society. You can find their page at www.paws.org/kids/.

They have their own group for kids like you called Kids Who Care, and if you get a group of friends together you can volunteer to help even if you are still under 18. E-mail (info@paws.org) or write to Progressive Animal Welfare Society, P.O. Box 1037, Lynnwood, WA 98046 for more information on their campaigns against circuses and ways you can support their campaigns.

Dress to a "T"

Question: Who designs the coolest clothes?
Answer: You! Equipped with paint, patches, colorful
  stitches, and positive be-kind-to-animals messages,
  your clothing will be truly one of a kind. Remember, compassion is the hippest fashion!

Did You Know?

- You can wear your heart on your sleeve (or on your knees, or on your back, or anywhere) as you spread animal rights messages without saying a word.
- Jazz up your jeans and your jacket! Put a raccoon patch on your coat that tells others SAVE OUR SKINS. Embroider your jeans with animals and mottoes like LOVE ANIMALS, DON'T EAT THEM and RATS HAVE RIGHTS!

🐾 You can do it yourself; it doesn't cost much to custom-make your own designer T-shirts, jeans, or jackets.

What You Can Do

Talk to your teacher and suggest that your whole class paint animal-friendly T-shirts as an art activity that will also help show all your friends—and your teacher too!—how easy it is to stand up for animals.

For your animal rights T-shirts, you may need to find or buy the following:

🐾 Plain all-cotton T-shirts. You can find them at almost any drugstore or department store, and the shirts are sometimes cheaper in packs of three.

🐾 Fabric ("textile") paints or waterproof fabric markers, which you can find at school or buy at art supply stores or fabric shops. Use paintbrushes, or get up to your elbows in paint and use your hands.

🐾 A wide piece of cardboard. If you don't have any at home, ask at a grocery store for a cardboard box.

Once you have the materials listed above, think of what you would like your T-shirt to show or say. You might want to try it on paper first so you'll have a good idea of what your design will look like before you put it on the shirt. Then you're ready to start! To make sure there are no wrinkles, "dress" the wide piece of cardboard with the T-shirt stretched out over it. By putting the piece of cardboard into the T-shirt, you can be sure that the colors will not seep through the fabric to stain the other side. It will also protect the table or whatever surface you are working on.

Be creative! You can paint, embroider, or design a patch with anything—a picture, a poem, or simply a kind message. Use your imagination!

Check It Out

- Look through books and magazines about animals to get ideas for designs to paint on your T-shirt and look at the pamphlets, magazines, bumper stickers, buttons, and posters of various animal protection organizations for mottoes and messages.
- If you need some inspiration for slogans and images for your T-shirt, check out the campaign pages and products at www.peta.org or www.petakids.com, where you will also find fun downloadable design stencils.
- If you want someone else to do the painting and patching for you, log on to www.customglam.com and www .neighborhoodies.com, which are two awesome sites you can use to design and order your own customized message on ultra-cool T-shirts, zip hoodies, polos—even underwear!

CHAPTER 23

Sing for the Animals

"I've always felt that animals are the purest spirits in the world. They don't fake or hide their feelings, and they are the most loyal creatures on Earth. And somehow we humans think we're smarter—what a joke!"

—P!nk

Did You Know?

- Everyone's musical. We all have drums in our ears!
- Lots of musicians incorporate animal sounds into their music, and some have made popular albums of this "interspecies"

music. You can also buy recordings of animal sounds, such as whales' songs and the sounds of birds and insects.

🐾 Some animal protection and environmental organizations have made record albums that feature popular musicians singing about animal abuse and our planet's fragile condition. Whether it's rock, jazz, or country, almost everyone likes and listens to music, and radio stations can reach millions of listeners.

🐾 In 2002, PETA teamed up with Fat Wreck Chords to put out the CD *Liberation* to raise awareness about animal rights and benefit PETA's campaigns. The CD features NOFX, The Used, Goldfinger, and The Faint, as well as an exclusive acoustic version of Good Charlotte's "Lifestyles of the Rich and Famous." The enhanced section of the CD also includes videos from Good Charlotte, Midtown, and Goldfinger, plus two popular PETA ads.

🐾 Hundreds of popular bands and musicians, like hot rocker P!nk, support animal rights and use their music to promote the issues to their listeners.

THEY SAID IT!

Here's what John Feldmann of Goldfinger has to say about how animals worked their way into his thoughts and into his songwriting:

"When my band was touring Europe in 1999, a truck-load of chickens passed our tour bus. . . . They were on the way to the slaughterhouse. A few miles down the road we stopped for food and the same truck of chickens was there. I stood outside the truck and listened to the chickens crying in fear. I felt so powerless. I was on my hands and knees crying because I could do nothing to change these peaceful, beautiful animals' fate. That night, I wrote 'Free Me.'"

Free Me

I didn't ask you to take me from here
I didn't ask to be broken
I didn't ask you to stroke my hair
or treat me like a worthless token

but my skin is thick
and my mind is strong
I am built like my father was
I've done nothing wrong

so free me
I just wanna feel what life should be
I just want enough space
to turn around
and face the truth
so free me . . .

. . . I just wanna feel what life should be
I just want enough space to turn around . . .
someday maybe you'll treat me like you

What You Can Do

🐾 Write your own songs about animals and the importance of protecting them. If you play an instrument or like to sing, take a leaf out of the songbook of cool and compassionate musicians like John Feldmann and write your own song for the animals. Decide on a topic—you might choose to sing the story of an animal on a factory farm, perhaps the story of how a fur collar got on someone's neck, or a happy song about how easy-peasy it is to live without hurting anyone, anytime, anywhere! So write away, right away!

🐾 Try out different styles of singing like rap, country, pop, hip-hop, or punk and find what works best for your lyrics. You might be surprised! And do share your creation with your friends or classmates when it's done so you are spreading the message of your song. You can also submit anything you've written to *Grrr!* or PETA Kids, who are always interested in the activities of caring kids like you. See www.petakids.com for exciting contest opportunities.

Check It Out

🐾 Try listening to musicians who are animal friendly. For tips on who they are, go to www.petakids.com, where you'll find a heap of interviews and photos of animal-friendly musos like Lindsay Lohan, rap legend Missy Elliott, Hilary Duff, Good Charlotte, Coldplay, and Avril Lavigne.

🐾 Call local radio stations to request animal rights songs like "Free Me" or songs from PETA's *Liberation* CD. If the station doesn't have the albums, tell the DJ you'd like to hear tunes from these fabulous albums in the future.

SHE DID IT!

When Cypress Bay High School sophomore Sara Schwartzman met Mandy Moore at a CD signing, the 16-year-old didn't just float away, star struck, with an autograph. She left a handful of anti-leather stickers and a Vegetarian Starter Kit with Mandy, who then mentioned that she wasn't really a "meat person" anyway. A huge 'N Sync fan, Sara also went to meet with band member Chris Kirkpatrick, known for his charity work, and talked with him about veganism, leaving him with a stack of PETA leaflets and a Vegetarian Starter Kit. She doesn't leave home without one.

🐾 If your favorite singers or bands haven't yet taken up animal issues, jot them a line or slip them an e-mail in care of their record label and encourage them to get involved. Send them information and names and addresses of animal rights organizations' Web sites and links to videos that will wake them up.

CHAPTER 24

Be an Elefriend—
Get the Elefacts

Bunny (who is actually an elephant!) was captured in Burma when she was just a baby and taken to a cramped exhibit cell at the Mesker Park Zoo in Indiana. Because Bunny had to sleep on hard concrete floors for almost 50 years, she developed painful wounds all over her body—imagine if someone stole you away from your mum and dad and made you sleep in a garage for half a century! Luckily she was rescued in 1999 and today she lives happily at the Elephant Sanctuary in Tennessee with a herd of other elephants who have been saved from lonely lives in zoos and circuses. Although most of her wounds have healed now, the scars will always be there, and Bunny will probably never forget how it felt to lose her big elephant family and exciting play times in the Asian jungle.

To find out how you can see Bunny and her friends playing at the sanctuary, go to "Check It Out" at the end of this chapter.

Did You Know?

- 🐾 Elephants can live to be seventy years old in their natural homes, but because of the ivory trade, fewer and fewer older elephants are found in Africa and Asia, where their homelands are.
- 🐾 Elephants have six sets of teeth during their life, while humans have only two, and elephants walk right on the tips of their toes.
- 🐾 Elephants are good swimmers and can use their trunks like a snorkel.
- 🐾 Elephant herds have a leader, usually the oldest and largest female. Female elephants stay with their families for their entire lives and males until they are 15 years old. Babies are raised by their mothers, aunts, and sometimes older sisters. Members of the elephant family look out for one another.
- 🐾 In 1988, a herd of elephants brought one of their babies to a park ranger's office for help. When the baby was hurt, the entire herd walked the two miles to the ranger's office where the baby could recover, safe from other dangers in the forest.
- 🐾 When poachers kill the adult elephants in a family for their tusks, they have little reason to kill the tuskless babies. Instead, the hunters tie up the young elephants, beat them until they stop fighting back (often called "breaking" an animal), and sell them to dealers, circuses, and zoos.

What You Can Do

- 🐾 Look out for anything made of ivory or elephant skin so you don't find yourself with a bangle or knickknack that took a life!

🐾 Be alert! Although bringing ivory into the United States is against the law, a lot of it is still around from before the ban. Tell stores that sell ivory that you don't want to shop in a store that sells bits of dead elephants no matter how old the tusks are.

🐾 Before buying anything that looks like ivory, be sure it's plastic. Lifesaving fake ivory is now popular to make piano keys (they used to be made of the real stuff) and is carved into ornaments, shaving brushes, and hairbrushes.

🐾 If you get a gift made of ivory, tell the giver that you appreciate the thought, but could they please exchange it for something else. Be sure to explain why.

🐾 Students at Valley Stream Elementary Schools, District 24, New York, built a four-foot-tall papier-mâché elephant that they wheel through the cafeteria during lunchtime. Calling the program Go Nuts for Elephants, students pay for a chance to guess how many peanuts are in a jar, and they win toy elephants for the closest guess. The students send the money they collect to their favorite group working to save the elephants. Perhaps you too can inform your friends and classmates about the dangers faced by elephants!

🐾 Say no to any visits to zoos, circuses, and other places that keep elephants in captivity, and never ride an elephant unless she can ride you back! Elephants should be free, roaming the land in Africa or in Asia that is protected from hunters.

🐾 Write to your members of Congress and ask them to give money to the people and organizations that are fighting poachers in Africa and Asia. Send your letter to the U.S. House of Representatives, Washington, DC 20510. Here's a sample letter:

Dear Representative [name],

I am writing to let you know that I am very concerned about elephants. They are being killed for their ivory, and because their natural habitat is being destroyed in Africa and Asia, I am afraid that by the time I'm old enough to vote, there may not be any elephants left to save. The ways they are killed are very cruel, and their bodies are left to rot. I hope you will vote for more tax money to be used to prevent elephant hunting and to protect their homelands so that the animals can live freely and the countries where they live can earn money from tourism. Thank you for remembering the elephants.

Sincerely,
[Your name]

Check It Out

- Watch Bunny and her elephant friends at the Elephant Sanctuary! Log on to www.tappedintoelephants.com and view a live-stream Web cam of them playing at home in Tennessee. For lots more stories about elephants like Bunny and ways you can help to save others, go to www.elephants.com or call the sanctuary at 931-796-6500.
- Visit www.petaliterature.com to download your free *Elephant Coloring Book* and Elefriend posters at www.petakids.com.
- Check out the Born Free Foundation's elephant site at www.bornfree.org.uk/elefriends/ and become a junior member for a small fee. You'll get your own Wild Crew membership card, certificate and Wild Crew poster as well as a Wild Crew folder and stickers, and regular Wild Crew activity sheets full of puzzles and animal facts. Write to Born Free Foundation, 3 Grove House, Foundry Lane, Horsham, West Sussex RH13 5PL UK or e-mail info@bornfree.org.uk.
- Write to the African Wildlife Foundation at 1400 Sixteenth St. N.W., Suite 120, Washington, DC 20036 or e-mail africanwildlife@awf.org to find out more about preserving elephants in the wild.

CHAPTER 25

Write On!

Question: What's black and white and read all over?
Answer: Your letters, of course!

Did You Know?

- Some cosmetics companies, such as Avon and Revlon, stopped testing on animals because they received so many letters asking them to.
- In 2005, the clothing company J.Crew decided to go fur free after receiving hundreds of protest letters from concerned kids.
- The television game show *Wheel of Fortune* stopped giving away fur coats as prizes after thousands of viewers protested in writing.
- Fifteen-year-old Jensen from Daytona, Florida, went to a Paul McCartney show and read his program, which featured the

letter Paul had written to KFC to protest their cruelty to chickens. Then she checked out www.peta.org as Paul suggested and went vegetarian after learning where (and who!) chicken nuggets actually come from.

🐾 Many people got upset and wrote to a company whose greeting cards had pictures of animals looking as if they were about to fall or be hurt. These letters made the company realize that people like to see pictures of happy animals and that putting animals in dangerous situations is no laughing matter!

🐾 Fourth-grader Clara Bird knows that even the tiniest animals deserve respect, including the mice her teacher was buying to feed to the classroom snake! "In the wild," she says, "the mice have a chance to escape from the snakes, but in the classroom, they were just put into the snake's cage until the snake ate them." Clara got her classmates to sign a letter urging the teacher to stop feeding the snake live animals.

🐾 A lot of magazines, newspapers, and companies have e-mail addresses too, so if you write a letter and mail it, make sure you e-mail the company a copy as well. If you have a personal page on a blog spot like www.myspace.com, use the messages you post to educate all the other kids who read it about the animal issues that matter. Put together a list of all your 'Net friends' e-mail addresses—that way you can let them all know in one hit exactly who deserves their protest letters. Ask them to forward the information on to all of their friends, too. You'll be amazed by how many people will read your message and send a letter by the end of even one day this way!

What You Can Do

The animals can't speak out for themselves, but lucky for them *you* can write against the wrongs!

🐾 Next time you and all your friends are arranging a get-together at someone's house, why not make it a great day for the animals too and suggest a "letter writing party." You can use colored paper, designer paper, old cards, or plain paper; the important thing is to put your thoughts down! Pick an issue for the night and help each other write protest letters. The more letters that get sent, the more the animals' voices get heard!

🐾 It's great if you can type your letters, but if you can't, who cares? You only need a pen and paper to send your messages of kindness. Make sure you write as neatly as you can—if busy people can't read the letter, they might throw it away. You might want to write a rough draft first; then, when you're really happy with what you want to say, copy the letter over, but don't worry too much about making it perfect. It *is* the thought that counts.

🐾 Perhaps you can write an article for your school newsletter. If your school doesn't have a paper, talk to a teacher about starting one. You could then devote an entire issue to animal abuse and—the best part—all the ways to help stop it! You can use information from animal protection groups to share the facts about animal experimentation, fur, and hunting. Include some easy vegetarian recipes!

🐾 Talk to your teacher(s) about toy and cosmetics companies who still test on animals.

Your class can write protest letters. Make sure to include the following:

🐾 Tell the company that you know there are much better ways than animal tests to make safe products. After all, lots of companies use alternatives such as human volunteers who let researchers put new products on the skin on their arms, for example, to see if it stings; natural ingredients from flowers and plants; ingredients we know are safe because people have been using them for years; and even artificial skin (this may sound kind of creepy, but it's not as creepy as using live rats, guinea pigs, and rabbits).

🐾 Ask the company to switch to modern, non-animal test methods. Many cruelty-free companies use very fancy computer programs that can tell in a split second (or less!) if an ingredient might harm a person's eyes or skin. So there's no excuse for blinding bunnies!

🐾 Let the company know you won't buy its products until it stops using animals (and that you'll tell others to boycott, too).

🐾 Ask for a reply to your letter. If you get a fuzzy response, or one you don't agree with, write all over again. That way they'll know you are serious. And, since, as the old saying goes, "the squeaky wheel gets the oil," be a squeaky wheel—let the company know you will keep right on writing until you're happy with their answer.

🐾 You can also send a polite letter of complaint to any and all stores that offer animal products, such as sheepskin coats, snakeskin clothing, and rabbits' feet. Let the store know you'll shop elsewhere until it stops selling such horrible things—and that you'll encourage others to do the same.

🐾 Make sure to write a few paragraphs in reply to any newspaper article about animal abuse. If the paper prints your letter, you'll reach many readers who might not know anything about this issue.

Here's a sample letter to the editor:

> Dear Editor,
>
> I read in your paper today that a balloon launch is to take place at the fair. Balloon launches may be pretty to watch, but the balloons don't just disappear into the clouds. They can end up in the oceans, where sea animals may swallow them. Thousands of sea turtles, dolphins, whales, and other creatures have died because they thought a floating balloon was food.

I hope that people will call the chamber of
commerce today to ask that the balloon launch be
called off before it is too late.

Sincerely,
[Your name]

🐾 If your town is planning events that include animal suffering
(such as a circus that uses animal acts), or if it offers carriage
horse rides, put your pen and paper to work, write a letter to
the newspaper(s) in your area and to your local chamber of
commerce (you can get the addresses from the phone book).
It's important that others know there are plenty of ways to
have fun without harming animals.

SHE DID IT!

One day Jenny Bain saw a booth at her local mall that was
selling hermit crabs with painted shells as pets for kids. She
knew that hermit crabs live on sandy beaches and that they
are very social and should never be kept alone, so she filled
out a comment card asking the mall to stop allowing the
kiosk to sell them. Jenny also sent a letter to the mall manager, telling him that her friends and family would not visit
the mall until the crab kiosk was gone. And she e-mailed
everyone she knew, telling them to stay away from the "live
novelty gifts" booth, and even contacted the company that
rents the kiosks with her protest. Boy, she was busy! A week
later, she received a phone call from the kiosk rental company. They told her that the crab booth's contract was up in
three days and that the mall would not be renting to them in
the future!

THEY SAID IT!

Some of the best celebrities do more than just sign autographs—they are also letter-writing champs when it comes to defending animals. Here are just a few of their achievements:

- P!nk sent a letter to Mayor Richard M. Daley in support of an elephant-protection law that would eliminate the use of elephants in Chicago's circuses by banning the use of bullhooks and electric prods. That law may have passed by now!
- Ryan Gosling, the Darkness, the Black Eyed Peas, and Jet *all* signed a letter to KFC's chief executive officer, David Novak, protesting the company's cruel abuse of chickens.
- Deryck, Steve, Dave, and Jay from Sum 41 wrote a letter to Canada's Manitoban minister of conservation, Oscar Lathlin, after learning that three Canadian polar bears had been captured and were being carted about in sizzling heat in the Suarez Brothers Circus. The polar bears were rescued from the circus and taken to a cold climate!
- Missy Elliott sent a letter to the vice-mayor of her hometown, Portsmouth, Virginia, to ask them to pass a law requiring that all animals adopted from any shelter be spayed or neutered, which would save thousands of lives. Woo-hoo—that law passed too!

🐾 Become an expert on how calves are raised for veal, how sled dogs are kept outside in the snow, how smart fish are, or on any animal protection issue, and earn an "A" at the same time: when it's time to write a report, choose an animal rights topic!

Check It Out

- Go to www.petakids.com and register for free e-mail alerts and your free copy of the cool kids' mag *Grrr!*—you'll be kept up to date with information on all the hot animal rights topics and which companies need to hear from you.
- Another great place to sign your name is at on-line petition sites. Petitions that are set up on the Internet often attract a lot of signatures because you can forward them to all your e-mail pals and get them to sign too! Check out www .thepetitionsite.com, where you can search for and sign petitions against animal cruelty and register for e-mail alerts when new petitions about animal issues are added.

CHAPTER 26

Born Free, Bored Stiff

A mother and baby camel are talking one day when the baby camel asks, "Mom, why have I got these huge three-toed feet?" The mother replies, "Well, son, when we trek across the desert your toes will help you to stay on top of the soft sand."

"Okay," said the son. A few minutes later the son asks, "Mom, why have I got these great long eyelashes?"

"They are there to keep the sand out of your eyes on the trips through the desert."

"Thanks, Mom," replies the son. After a short while, the son returns and asks, "Mom, why have I got these great big humps on my back?" The mother, now a little impatient with the son, replies, "They are there to help us store water for our long treks across the desert, so we can go without drinking for long periods."

"That's great, Mom. So we have huge feet to stop us sinking, and long eyelashes to keep the sand from our eyes, and these humps to store water—but Mom . . ."

"Yes, son?"

"Why are we in the zoo?"

Did You Know?

🐾 Zoos started long ago as menageries, collections of "exotic" wild animals kept by kings and emperors. Then showmen decided the public might pay to see "fierce" tigers, "weird" monkeys, and other "odd" creatures they couldn't find close to home, so city zoos were built. Collectors went to Africa, South America, and Asia to catch animals the public would ooh and aah over.

🐾 Today, most zoos and marine parks are sad places for animals: simply museums of living beings kept in cement pens and cages or in small pools or outdoor enclosures. Although they get basic food and water, most of the animals don't have much to do and must be going out of their minds with boredom.

🐾 Often, when animals have been in their small enclosures at the zoo for too long, they go "stir crazy" and start pacing up and down or whirling around in circles or they start swaying back and forth, over and over again, in their cages. Sometimes they even bite and chew at their own arms or legs or pull their hair out. This is a form of madness that happens when the animals become crazy from being so bored and sad because they have been taken away from their exciting natural environment and social activities.

🐾 Animals who live where they belong, at home in the jungle, forest, ocean, or desert, stay busy building their own dens, nests, or burrows, sniffing the ground and the air for the latest news, and searching for foods they like. They raise their families and stay active in their community.

🐾 Orcas (also known as "killer whales" because they hunt for live fish) can live to be eighty years old. But, from the time they are captured, those at marine parks only survive from eighteen months to twenty years, just a quarter of their natural lifespan, tops.

🐾 Some bottlenose dolphins have developed ulcers because of the stress of being on display. It upsets them to have noisy crowds staring at them all the time with no place to hide. Since dolphins use sonar to communicate, they become confused when it bounces off the walls of their tiny enclosures (it must feel a bit like being surrounded by mirrors all the time).

🐾 Many animals are taken from their faraway homes and shipped in small crates to zoos. It's hard to lure baby animals away from their protective families and friends, so sometimes adult members of the community or family are killed. For example, mother chimpanzees and older relatives are often shot so collectors can capture their children.

🐾 When zoos end up with more animals than they want of one species, and when animals grow old, some zoos sell the animals directly, or through dealers and auctions, to people who own "game farms" where people can pay to shoot them. That way they can put the animals' heads on their walls and pretend to have been in a daring adventure. Other animals end up badly neglected at small roadside zoos.

🐾 Pole Pole (whose name is pronounced "polly polly" and means "slowly slowly" in the African language Swahili) was a baby elephant who was captured to appear in a movie. Her "acting" days ended very quickly, and she was sent to the London Zoo. There she rocked back and forth and banged her head on the bars, trying to escape into a dream world in order not to think about her frustrating life in the concrete prison. She watched as her elephant friends either died or were sent away. Although some people cared enough to fight to improve her life, the plans to finally move Pole Pole to a better park were made too late. After years of sadness, Pole

Pole, who was only a teenager of seventeen years, lay down for the last time, having lost her will to live.

What You Can Do

- Stay away from zoos, aquariums, or marine parks. If people don't go to them, they won't make any money and will have to close down, which means animals will get to stay in their homes.
- Stay away from dolphin swim programs, too. Just say "Thanks, but no tanks!" It may sound like fun to swim with dolphins in a pool, but it can be dangerous to both the dolphins and the people swimming about with them. If swim programs become popular, more dolphins will be captured. Dolphins, who are stronger swimmers than humans, have slapped people with their tails and rammed them with their noses. Although the dolphins probably don't mean to hurt swimmers, they can become frustrated and angry. Plus, dolphins can catch human diseases. Your cold could make a dolphin very sick.
- If your class is planning a field trip to the zoo, ask your teacher to plan a trip to a museum, park, sanctuary, or cave instead. If your teacher or family insists that you go to the zoo, be sure to bring along a pencil and paper to take notes (and a camera, if you can). Keep your eyes open for the following:
  - Do the animals have water? Is it clean? Are there shady trees they can lie down under?
  - Do they have company?
  - Can they stand up, lie down, and move around comfortably?
  - How much space do they have to run and roam in? Can they get to private space when they want to escape the stares of the gawking visitors?
  - Are the animals active? Are they running, playing, or climbing? Do they have toys?

- Do the animals look healthy? Are their coats shiny (a sign of wellness)?
- Do they have any sores or injuries?
- Does the area smell? Because of bad zoos and kennels, people sometimes expect animal places to smell, but they shouldn't if the caretakers are doing their jobs well!

Different animals have special needs that need to be met:

🐾 Check to see if the great apes are in family groups. Do they have things to do? Or are they in small areas, with nothing to do but be stared at, eat, and fall asleep?

🐾 Do the elephants and other large animals have rubbing posts and pools in their pens?

🐾 Do the birds have at least two separate perches or roosts? Or can they only fly into walls, fences, or onto the floor if frightened?

They Did It!

🐾 After reading information from PETA about the Three Bears Gift Shop in Tennessee where bears are kept in a depressing concrete pit and often don't even have clean food or drinking water, 12-year-old Cory Cummings created a Web site to get the word out about the animals' miserable living conditions. You can check out Cory's site at (www.webspawner .com/users/nagelnighthawk), which has already received hundreds of hits!

🐾 Vegan high school student Danielle Lanz contacted PETA for help after learning that she had to study zoos for the last semester of her science class. She was required to take a field trip to the Columbus Zoo and then had to design a zoo as her final project. After speaking to her teacher about the plight of zoo animals, she was allowed to design a sanctuary and rehabilitation center instead. She didn't go on the field trip and still received an A in the class! Way to go, Danielle!

Check It Out

🐾 Because of Pole Pole's sad life, a group called Zoo Check was formed to help inform the public about the problems with zoos. You can find Zoo Check at www.bornfree.org.uk/zoocheck/ and e-mail zoocheck@bornfree.org.uk for a Zoo Check information pack or write to Zoo Check (c/o Born Free Foundation, 3 Grove House, Foundry Lane, Horsham, West Sussex RH13 5PL, UK). Another organization called Zoocheck who campaign for animals in captivity is Zoocheck Canada. You can find out more about them at www.zoocheck.com (e-mail: zoocheck@zoocheck.com) or by writing to 2646 St. Clair Ave., East Toronto, ON M4B 3M1, Canada.

🐾 For a more detailed zoo checklist, contact the Animal Welfare Institute (AWI). Check out www.awionline.org, e-mail awi@awionline.org or write to P.O. Box 3650, Washington, DC 20007.

🐾 For lots of information about dolphins and ways to help them, log on to www.paws.org/kids/wildlife/marine_mammals.html, the Progressive Animal Welfare Society's kids' pages.

🐾 Log on to PETA's Web site www.zooinsiders.com, where you can read a checklist of things to look out for at zoos and how to report things you might see. You can report your concerns by calling 1-866-ZOO-TIPS, the bad zoo tip-off hotline.

🐾 You can watch live animals without supporting the cruelty of zoos: log on to www.tappedintoelephants.com and watch a live-stream Web cam of happy animals at the Elephant Sanctuary in Tennessee, which gives a home to the lucky elephants saved from zoos and circuses. See Chapter 24, "Be an Elefriend—Get the Elefacts," for more stories about the elephants who live there.

CHAPTER 27

Saying Good-Bye to Uninvited Guests

Monty: "Aren't you gonna run?"
Stuart Little: "Why?"
Monty: "'Cause you're a mouse."
Stuart Little: "I'm not just a mouse. I'm a member
of this family!"

—*Stuart Little,* the movie

Two cockroaches were munching snacks on top of a garbage pile when one of them began telling his friend about some new people on the block: "I hear their refrigerator is spotless, their floors gleaming, and there is not a speck of dust in the place."

"Please," said the other cockroach, "not while I'm eating!"

Sometimes the tiniest of creatures wanders or flaps into our

THEY SAID IT!

The Olsen twins have a heart for flies:

Ashley told *Rolling Stone*, "I don't kill spiders, because I always feel bad." Pointing to Mary-Kate, she said, "I remember years ago, when I swatted a fly, you said, "'What if it had a brother or a sister? Do you know how sad the other would be?'"

homes. It is usually a mistake, but mistakes can have a happy ending with a little help from us. Animals need our respect and understanding when they are in our houses—frightened and probably wanting very badly to get back outdoors where their homes and families are.

Did You Know?

- Grasshoppers can jump up to thirty inches at a time. If we were that strong, we could jump a football field in one leap!
- Ants can lift more than fifty times their own body weight.
- Squirrels plant trees. How? Because they bury so many nuts and seeds in the summer and fall that some of them sprout into trees!
- Bats are the only mammals who fly with wings of skin, not feathers. They use radar vision to tell how far away an object is, but they can also tell, if the light is right, just by looking.

Do Unto Others

Live by the Golden Rule: "Do unto others as you would have them do unto you." When dealing with any lost or confused animals, try to put yourself in their place. Imagine being a frightened little spider, mouse, squirrel, bat, bird, or insect, and help them as you would want to be helped. Remember that they are afraid of people (after all, to them we look as big as a battleship looks to us) and treat them gently and calmly whenever you come across them.

Bats in Your Belfry?

If bats come into your house, don't be afraid! Bats are very sensitive and gentle animals who do not get caught in people's hair! That's an old wives' tale. If they get into your home, turn off all the lights and open the doors and windows. They will probably find their own way out. If not, catch them very gently, by putting a large jar over them or a plastic trash bin. Be very careful not to hurt them and ask an adult to help you. Try never to pick them up, as scared bats may bite.

Bird in Your Bedroom?

If you find a bird trapped in your house, ever so gently corner him or her in one room with a window to the outside world. Close off the room from the rest of the house and open the window all the way. You should leave the room, so the bird feels safe enough to look for a way out. Don't be impatient—as long as the bird isn't hurt, he or she will find the window sooner or later. If the bird has not left by evening, hang a light outside the window and turn off all the lights in the room. The bird will fly toward the outside light. Prevent other birds and bugs from getting caught in your house in the future by keeping screens on your windows.

Birds can't see glass, and sometimes they fly into windows and hurt themselves, but you can prevent those sore heads and dazed birds:

🐾 If you have a large picture window or sliding glass doors, warn birds not to fly into them by cutting long thin strips of cloth (about one-half-inch wide) and placing them about four inches apart so they hang down in front of the window (thanks for this tip go to Carroll Henderson of the Minnesota Department of Natural Resources).

Mouse in Your House?

You can help mice move out by using a "humane" box mousetrap, which allows you to release the mice, totally unharmed, outside. When catching mice with a humane trap, follow these guidelines:

- ❀ Set the trap somewhere dark where you think the mice are hanging around (perhaps inside a kitchen cabinet where you have seen mouse droppings). Put a little blob of peanut butter in the trap to attract the mice. Everyone loves peanut butter!
- ❀ Check the trap every hour. If mice are left in the trap for too long, they get very thirsty and scared and could hurt themselves. Once mice are caught, rush them to a field near your house, where there are lots of bushes and plants for them to hide under. If you have more than one mouse, try to take them all to the same place so they can be together.
- ❀ Don't catch mice in the winter. They could freeze when suddenly put outside, as they are used to indoor living! Wait until spring or summer.
- ❀ Always remember that mice and other little animals are very afraid of people and very, very afraid of loud noises. In fact, they "speak" so softly that you can't usually hear them at all without very sensitive recording equipment. When you catch a mouse, be very careful carrying the trap and move very quietly, too. Place the trap gently on the ground when setting the animal free, and don't make any clatter or fast, scary movements. You can wave good-bye, though!

Befriend a Bug!

Flies, moths, spiders, and other insects can be helped home with these ideas:

- ❀ Keep a bug-release kit handy so you can return these small animals to the outside where they belong. All you need is a see-through glass with a wide opening and a stiff piece of paper or cardboard—period!

🐾 Wait until the insect is resting to put the cup over him/her, but watch out for little legs and delicate wings! Gently slide the cardboard underneath. Just be patient, and eventually you'll get the bug into the cup. Then you can release him or her back into the great outdoors.

Cockroaches and Ants Get Hungry Too!

Cockroaches and ants come into our houses for the same reasons mice do: they can't resist food crumbs. In addition to keeping food in sealed containers and wiping up crumbs, you can also try these tricks:

🐾 Wash countertops, cabinets, and floors with a solution of vinegar and water—the same amount of each—to keep ants on the march.

🐾 Place whole bay leaves in several spots around the kitchen (you can find bay leaves with the other herbs and seasonings at the grocery store). Bay leaves smell to cockroaches like old socks do to us, and they'll avoid them. Change them every couple of months or so.

🐾 Pour a line of cream of tartar (in the baking aisle at the grocery store) at the ants' entrance. They won't cross the line.

🐾 Always look in the bathtub before you turn on the shower. It helps to have your clothes on because you may have to run outside with a moth or a spider!

Don't Do It!

Never use any kind of sticky glue trap. These traps are very cruel, causing the animals to get their feet, tails, and even their faces stuck in the sticky goo. If you see that someone has put out glue traps, ask the person who has set them if they will please immediately throw them away. Explain what awful things they are and suggest that they use more humane methods to ward off unwanted visitors. Offer to help pick them up, squash the gluey bits together so that they are safe, and take them to the trash.

What You Can Do

🐾 If you have to move mice, ask your parents to get only humane traps or, better yet, use deterrents. There are a lot more kind methods of controlling uninvited houseguests. There are electronic devices that produce high-pitched sounds you can't hear but the insects hate and so they head for the hills. There is also the Katcha Bag, a humane bug catcher. And mice won't die with the Smart Mousetrap, which keeps mice safe in a little house until you release them back into the outdoors. You can find out more about these products and order them at www.petacatalog.org, or by calling PETA at 757-622-PETA.

🐾 Log on to www.peta.org and read or request the fact sheet *Compassionate Lawn Care* about local animals who might be harmed by gardening chemicals. Make sure your parents are aware that more than the grass needs to survive.

🐾 Ask your teacher to visit the Share the World site (www .sharetheworld.com) and use some of the suggestions there for classroom activities. Share the World is a free educational program designed to help kids get to know and care about the animals with whom we share our world, and it gives good ideas about what to do when animals are in trouble.

Check It Out!

🐾 Watch the movies *Stuart Little* and *Stuart Little 2*, which tell the story of a tiny mouse with a big personality who is adopted by a human family. Bet you'll never look at mice in quite the same way again!

- Write to Rat Allies (P.O. Box 3453, Portland, OR 97208) or call 503-287-7894 to find out how you can help improve the image of these unfairly treated animals.
- Contact Bat Conservation International to learn more about these curious little flying mammals. Up close, they look like upside-down Chihuahuas. You can find the group at www.batcon.org, or write to P.O. Box 162603, Austin, TX 78716-2603, or e-mail batinfo@batcon.org.

CHAPTER 28

Talk to the Animals

A stranger came into a restaurant. At the next table sat a dog and a cat. As the stranger sat down, the dog rose, yawned, and said, "Well, so long," and walked out.

The stranger's jaw dropped. He said to the waiter, "Did you hear that? The dog talked."

"Don't be a fool," said the waiter. "A dog can't talk."

"But I heard him."

"You just think you heard him. I tell you dogs can't talk. It's just that wiseguy cat over there. He's a ventriloquist."

Except in cartoons and on TV shows, animals don't usually speak in our language, but they do know how to talk in their own way. For several years, a professor named C. N. Slobodchikoff and his students have been using high-tech equipment to listen to what prairie dogs say in a field in Arizona. They've found that the "voice prints" of prairie dogs show different barks in response to the size, shape, and even color of the fur, skin, or clothing of coyotes, snakes, and humans going by!

Did You Know?

🐾 Washoe, one of a family of chimpanzees who has been taught American Sign Language, was raised in a human home. She makes up words for objects she has never seen before. She came up with "water fruit" for watermelon. The first time she bit into a radish she signed, "hurt cry food." Washoe has taught her adopted chimpanzee son, Loulis, more than seventy of the hundreds of signs she knows, including a name for himself, which is a rub-your-head kind of sign.

🐾 When a little kitten bit Koko, an enormous gorilla who also knows sign language, Koko signed, "Cat real bad Koko. Teeth visit gorilla!" and gently put the kitten onto the ground. When Washoe first saw another ape, a chimpanzee, she was frightened and signed, "big black bug."

🐾 Talk about making long-distance "caws": crows in the south of France have a different "accent" from crows in the north!

🐾 Lawrence Kilham, who observed crows for seven years, would often give them corn. On days when he didn't feed them, crows would walk behind him and peck at the bare ground whenever he turned around to let Kilham know they wanted to eat!

🐾 Some believe that dolphins can actually read other dolphins' minds. Their language is made up of "click" sounds—as many as seven hundred a second—and some marine mammal experts believe dolphins can send whole pictures of what they see to other dolphins, just as we see images on a TV screen sent from a station miles away!

🐾 Bees "speak" by dancing. They use different wing flaps to give complicated directions to hive members, allowing them to find flowers miles and miles away!

What You Can Do

If you have a dog or other companion animal, practice good communication skills with her or him:

- Are your "conversations" with your dog, cat, or other companions one-sided? When you talk to them, is it only to give commands like "No," "Sit," or "Stay"? Do your animal companions feel as if they are in the army? Oh, no! It's really important to give them the time and the freedom to express their feelings. See if you can figure out what they are "saying" with their eyes, ears, paws, tails, and voices. For example, what are dogs trying to tell us to do when they put a paw on our knees or keep going to the door and then looking back at us? Did you know that when cats make their tails into a question mark they are telling us that they are happy? Just as when a dog puts his tail between his legs it means he is sending us a message that he is scared and would rather you didn't hurt him! Do you try to answer the right way?

- Watch for your animals' "body language" and answer it as best you can. Even if you aren't sure what your animal friends are trying to tell you, respond to them. Stroke them on the head or say, "What is it?" so that they know you aren't ignoring them.

- How many different sounds does your animal friend make? Can you tell the difference between a happy, excited "I missed you" bark, a "Please let me out, it's urgent!" bark, and a bark warning you that "Hey, someone's coming to the door"? Cats have lots of "voices," too. How many can you recognize?

- Dogs appreciate knowing the rules—it makes their lives easier. But since you speak a foreign language to them, be very patient. After all, if we had to bark or mew to get what we wanted, we'd be stuck! Always use the same word and the same tone for something you want them to learn, or you'll confuse them. Oh, and never raise your voice or your hand to them, or they'll be too upset to learn a thing.

Check It Out

🐾 For tips on how to talk to and train a companion dog, look for a copy of *Mother Knows Best: The Natural Way to Train Your Dog* by Carol Lea Benjamin (Howell Book House, Inc., 1985) or *Communicating with Your Dog: A Humane Approach to Dog Training* by Ted Baer (Barton's Educational Series, 1989). There are also lots of other books about communicating with animals. Just a few of these are *Animals Are Smarter than Jack* by Jenny Campbell, *Bees Dance and Whales Sing: The Mysteries of Animal Communication* by Margery Facklam, *Minding Animals* by Mark Bekoff, *Conversations with Dog: An Uncommon Dogalog of Canine Wisdom* and *Conversations with Cat: An Uncommon Catalog of Feline Wisdom* by Kate Solisti-Mattelon, *What Your Dog Is Trying to Tell You* by John M. Simon, *How to Talk to Your Dog* by Jean Craighead George.

🐾 If you have a cat, you (and your cat!) will love *250 Things You Can Do to Make Your Cat Adore You* by the same author as this book. It gives you hundreds of ways to show your kitty how much you care, including fun games, facts, and toys to make.

🐾 Write Friends of Washoe to request their newsletter, buy prints by Washoe, or buy a T-shirt with a picture of Washoe on it. You can find them at www.friendsofwashoe.org or write to Chimpanzee and Human Communication Institute, Central Washington University (400 E. University Way, Ellensburg, WA 98926-7573) or by e-mail at mougk@cwu .edu. On their Web site you can also watch a live Web cam of the chimpanzees in their play areas!

🐾 Watch the movies *Dr. Doolittle* (1998) and *Dr. Doolittle 2* (2001), which star Eddie Murphy as a doctor who suffers a knock to the head in a car accident and finds out he can then have conversations with animals! Enjoy all his exciting adventures in the animal kingdom and discover what the animals teach *him* about being human.

🐾 If you've ever wondered what the animals might say if they could talk our language, you'll enjoy a Claymation cartoon series called *Creature Comforts* (Aardman Animations, 2003), which is available on DVD. It comes from the makers of Wallace and Gromit and shows cats, dogs, hamsters, fish, aliens, horses, and many other animals (in zoos, in houses, and in the wild) being interviewed about the issues that are closest to their hearts.

CHAPTER 29

Get Your Class into the Act

Liven up your class with animals—never in terrariums or cages, or on cutting boards, of course, poor things, but in books and magazines, through projects and papers, in videos and filmstrips, through actions you take, and in everyone's imagination.

Did You Know?

🐾 Animals don't belong in the classroom. We can't learn much from captive critters—except that rats, mice, rabbits, guinea pigs, gerbils, hamsters, and turtles get bored and lonely in aquariums!

SHE DID IT!

Skylar Chissell has been active for animals her whole life. That's a photo of her at the top of this chapter! She went (with her mother) to her very first demonstration against fur when she was only a tiny baby. Now Skylar passes out PETA stickers and comic books at show-and-tell, lets her classmates share some of the great food she eats because she is a vegan, and carries a lunchbox that is printed with the message ANIMALS ARE NOT OURS TO EAT.

🐾 It doesn't make scientific sense to use rats in nutrition experiments in class: Rats don't make good "models" of what happens when kids eat the wrong foods. For one thing, rats can actually make their own vitamin C in their bodies, but humans have to get vitamin C by eating it in their food; and rats need from 3½ to 10 times *more* protein than kids.

🐾 When Jamie, Kristina, and Gemma London's elementary school held a jump-roping fund-raiser for the American Heart Association, the teacher meant well, but didn't know that this charity gives money to researchers who test on animals! "Yuck!" said the kids, who decided to "skip" it and teach everyone a lesson in kindness by raising money for PETA or any other worthy, cruelty-free organizations instead.

What You Can Do

🐾 Ask for a class field trip to a local farm, animal sanctuary, or animal shelter to see how animals are cared for, learn what calves or chickens lives are really like, or find out how you and your class can help injured or stray animals. Write about what you think you'll see before you go and, afterwards, write what you did see. You may be very surprised!

If your class can't go someplace special, bring something special to your classroom or auditorium!

🐾 Martita Goshen has a dance program just for kids. Her dance themes include elephants, the ocean, and Africa, and she travels all over the country to show her love of animals and nature to students through dance. Your teacher(s) can write to her at Turtles, Inc., 111 Carpenter Ave., Sea Cliff, NY 11579.

🐾 To arrange a singing or storytelling program about treating the world and its inhabitants more thoughtfully, you might suggest that your teacher contact Sisters' Choice (1450 Sixth St., Berkeley, CA 94710). Nancy Schimmel (a storyteller) and Candy Forest (a singer) travel around the country giving performances to kids of all ages and workshops to people age nine and up. You can find out more at www.sisterschoice.com.

🐾 Singer-songwriter David Williams performs lots of songs about animals for kids, some of which are recorded on a tape called *Oh, The Animals!* To invite Mr. Williams to your school, ask your teacher to write to him at Trapdoor Records, P.O. Box 5584, Springfield, IL 62705, or visit www.trapdoormedia.com/html/kids/ohtheanimals.html.

🐾 Members of Youth for Environmental Sanity travel everywhere (on the YES! tour) giving very lively presentations and getting whole assemblies involved in workshops at schools. For more information, visit www.yesworld.org, write to YES!, 420 Bronco Rd., Soquel, CA 95073, or e-mail camps@yesworld.org, or phone 831-465-1091.

🐾 If your school has a video camera available for loan, or if you have a family camera, maybe you could use it to produce your own TV-style news with reports about animal issues. You could interview visitors to the zoo to see what they think about seeing animals so far from their native homes, or feature a dog or cat who is waiting for a home at a shelter. For ideas, and to view some really wild animal TV reports, log on to www.petatv.com or www.animal-tv.org.

🐾 Check out the education program set up by Share the World (www.sharetheworld.com) and suggest to your teacher that your whole class could do one of the activities as a group. There are lots of downloadable work sheets with super ideas, like putting together a list of what neat inventions might replace animals, just as in the old days horses who had to pull heavy loads were glad to lose their jobs to trucks! That could get everyone thinking creatively about all the ways animals are still used, and how to help them.

🐾 Another idea is to gather brochures, posters, books, and information on a particular topic and ask if you can put up a lovely display in your school or local library. Hundreds of people will become informed on the subject of your choice (For example, what incredible songs birds sing, how much more food an animal needs if he or she is outside in winter, or how bees give complicated directions to other bees so they can find flowers) and will probably check out the books that are featured in the display too.

🐾 When choosing subjects for school reports, suggest animals many people misunderstand, like rats, snakes, bats, wolves, or octopuses. Make yourself the local expert on one of these animals. You can be the ambassador for that species—let them be your theme for projects and sing their praises through your art and words!

Check It Out

Get competitive! Have the whole class enter a contest for the animals. Here are some ideas:

🐾 Visit the www.petakids.com Web site for on-line petitions and competitions and check out the current edition of the *PETA* Kids mag, *Grrr!* Suggest your class take out a subscription to *Grrr!* so you can find out about future art, design, and writing competitions to enter.

🐾 Contact the Kindness Club for information regarding their annual essay contest for their members in the fifth through the eighth grade. Check out www.kindnessclub.nb.ca, write to the Kindness Club, 65 Brunswick St. Fredericton NB E3B 1G5, Canada, or e-mail kindness@nb.aibn.com.

🐾 Contact the Vegetarian Resource Group about their annual essay contest for students. Check out the Web site at www.vrg .org, or write to VRG, P.O. Box 1463, Baltimore, MD 21203.

Ask each person in your class to contribute fifty cents toward a class membership to an animal protection group or have a fund-raiser such as a bake sale or a car wash to cover the membership cost:

🐾 A subscription with the National Association for Humane and Environment Education entitles a class to thirty-two copies of each bimonthly issue of *Kind News Junior* (grades two to four) or *Kind News Senior* (grades five to six). Write to NAHEE, 67 Norwich Essex Turnpike, East Haddam, CT 06423-1736, or e-mail nahee@nahee.org. You can find out more at www.nahee.org.

🐾 Your teacher can write to the American Humane Education Society (AHES), at 350 South Huntington Ave., Boston, MA 02130 or call 1-800-AHES-929 for information on Operation Outreach USA.

🐾 Borrow or buy the twenty-minute videotape *Kept in the Dark*, about a class of British schoolkids who learn the difference between "open air" and "factory" farming. You can order it from Compassion in World Farming. Visit www.ciwf.org.uk, or write to Charles House, 5a Charles St., Petersfield, Hampshire, GU32 3EH, UK.

🐾 Your class can "adopt" a wolf at Wolf Haven America, a sanctuary that provides care and protection for these animals. You will receive a photograph of and adoption certificate for the wolf whose life you help to improve. You will also receive a subscription to the sanctuary's newsletter. Their Web site is www.wolfhaven.org, or you can write to them at

3111 Offutt Lake Rd., Tenino, WA 98589, or call toll free
1-800-448-9653.

🐾 Suggest to your teacher that your class could foster an orphaned baby elephant or orangutan through the Orangutan
Foundation International, the David Sheldrick Wildlife Trust,
or the Elephant Sanctuary. You'll receive photos, videos, and
updates on your adopted baby as well as information on the
exotic animal trade and how to protest it. To find out more,
go to www.sheldrickwildlifetrust.org, www.orangutan.org,
or www.elephants.com. You can also write to the Orangutan
Fund International (4201 Wilshire Blvd., Suite 407, Los Angeles, CA 90010) or call 1-800-ORANGUTAN. To foster an
elephant, write to the David Sheldrick Wildlife Trust (P.O. Box
15555, Nairobi, Kenya) or e-mail rc-h@africaonline.co.ke,
and for the Elephant Sanctuary, e-mail elephants@elephant
.com or call 931-796-6500.

CHAPTER 30

Hooray for Holidays!

On the first day of summer vacation, a duck, a frog, and a skunk decided to go to the movies. The duck could afford the ticket because he had a "bill," and so could the frog because he had a "greenback." But the skunk only had a "scent" and had to wait outside!

Everybody likes vacations, holidays, and special occasions. These special times are also a great time to remember the animals, too. Sometimes there are so many other things going on that we tend to forget them, but animals can make our celebrations that much more joyous.

Did You Know?

🐾 If a cockroach got cards from all her sons and daughters on Mother's Day, she could have over 300 of them!

🐾 On October 5, Catholics celebrate Saint Francis Day. Saint Francis of Assisi is the patron saint of all animals because he cared for them so much.

🐾 Not only is October your chance to dress up as your fave animal and have a cruelty-free-candy-filled Halloween, it is also Cut Out Dissection Month and Vegetarian History Month. Check out www.petakids.com and www.peta.org for information and activities planned to celebrate these events. At PETA Kids there is even an interactive calendar on-line that lists the animal events for each month with links to further information. You'll also find holiday themed e-cards, which you can send out to all your friends!

What You Can Do

🐾 Raccoons love Halloween so much they wear their masks all year round! This Halloween, dress up as an animal. What would it be like to have an elephant's long trunk or a polar bear's thick coat? Do you need to practice a new way of walking on four "legs" or holding things in your "paws"? You could hold or wear a sign with an animal rights message like LOVE THE SKIN YOU'RE IN!

🐾 On Valentine's Day, remember your companion animals with a warm hug and a kiss. Send valentines (little dog treats) to the animals and a card to the people who work at your local animal shelter.

🐾 If people you know are thinking of giving or getting chicks or baby rabbits for Easter (or any other holiday), let them know that humane societies end up with lots of these animals, not always in great shape, after the holidays. Tell them plush animal toys or flowering plants (which don't need to be kept warm and fed every hour!) would be much better.

🐾 Think of companion animals on the Fourth of July, when they may be frightened by the sounds of firecrackers. It helps to sit with them, stroke them, talk to them quietly, and play soothing music on the radio to drown out bangs. You can also teach a timid dog not to be frightened by loud noises. Choose a special word or phrase to say to your dog each time there's a worrying noise (like thunder). Say it in a really upbeat way—with the same tone of voice you would use to say, "Isn't this great?" Once you get your dog to respond to you (with a wag of the tail or whatever), praise him or her lavishly. With a little luck, you may be able to get your dog to think that loud noises are not going to hurt her.

🐾 This Thanksgiving, ask if your family can enjoy a vegetarian meal that helps us give thanks for life in *all* its wonderful forms. Did you know that in the wild (where turkeys are brown or black, not white) these amazing birds can run up to eighteen miles per hour and fly even faster; and that wild turkeys flatten themselves against trees when they hear hunters coming? Who can miss munching on a turkey when there's corn chowder, tofu loaf, harvest stuffing, and pumpkin pie to enjoy instead?

🐾 The next time you're in the market for a birthday, Christmas, or Hanukkah gift, think about buying some cruelty-free lotions, a toy that has not been tested on animals, a "pleather" (short for "plastic leather") belt, or some funky vegan foods. For the person who has everything, make the gift twice as good by making a donation in her or his name to an organization that helps animals, like a donkey sanctuary or chimpanzee refuge or the local animal shelter.

🐾 Get your school or family to celebrate Arbor Day (usually the last Friday in April) by planting a tree. In a year or two, up to 40 animals will have made a home in it! You can choose a tree, like an evergreen or spruce, that will make a good home for sparrows, finches, and starlings; or a food shrub, like a viburnum, whose fruits will provide much-needed winter meals for local wildlife when the cold weather comes. Squirrels, raccoons, opossums, moths, birds, worms, and frogs are some of the many animals who might eventually make a home in the tree you plant.

Take out your calendar and add some new holidays:

🐾 Your animal friend's birthday! If you aren't sure of the date, choose one (he or she isn't picky about things like that!) and celebrate it every year as you would any family birthday.

🐾 Join in the Great American Meat-Out (March 21). Every year, this group encourages people to kick that habit and stop eating meat for a day (or a lifetime!) just to see how easy it is. For more information go to www.meatout.org or call 1-800-MEATOUT.

🐾 Observe World Week for Animals in Laboratories (the fourth week in April). During this week, people all over the world hold rallies, give speeches, and meet to let others know what happens to animals in laboratories and how simply choosing a shampoo that isn't tested on animals or asking for a computer program instead of dissecting a frog helps. Check it out at www.wwail.org.

🐾 Check with local animal rights groups for any activities they may have planned for special days.

🐾 If you know of someone who is getting married soon, you can give the couple a great gift that is really for the birds! Cut up squares of pretty fabric and put a handful of birdseed in each square. Then tie up the squares with colorful ribbon to make little sacks. Save them to distribute to the guests when the couple is about to leave, so that people can empty the birdseed into their hands and throw it over the newlyweds instead of rice, which can swell up inside birds' stomachs and make them sick.

Check It Out

- For holiday recipes, contact the Vegetarian Resource Group (check out the Web site at www.vrg.org, and write to VRG, P.O. Box 1463, Baltimore, MD 21203) or *Vegetarian Times* (www.vegetariantimes.com or write to P.O. Box 420235, Palm Coast, FL 32142-0235).

- Just because you're saving the turkey's life at Thanksgiving certainly doesn't mean you'll go hungry or miss out on tradition, thanks to the Tofurky Roast, a pre-cooked vegetarian feast designed to be the delicious centerpiece of your holiday meal. Made from a revolutionary tofu-wheat protein blend, Tofurky even won America's Favorite Meat Substitute Award! For find out more visit www.tofurkey.com and check out the complete products list at the end of this book.

- Write or call Seventh Generation (www.seventhgeneration.com, 1-800-456-1177) for a catalog of environmentally friendly gifts, or write to PETA for a catalog of cruelty-free and animal rights merchandise. You can check out all their exciting merchandise as well as links to other animal-friendly stores at www.petamall.com.

- Look at books on how to make costumes. *Illegally Easy Halloween Costumes for Kids* by Leila Peltosaari (2001) includes illustrated instructions for making many animal costumes such as mice, lions, lobsters, and chickens. Your library might have even more, similar books on hand.

- Read *The Christmas Cat*, written by Esther Tudor Holmes, illustrated by Tasha Tudor (Crowell, New York, 1976). You might also like *Mog's Christmas* by Judith Kerr, *Twelve Days of a Feline Christmas* by Betty Linkinhoker, or *A Cat's Night Before Christmas* by Henry Beard.

🐾 If you're after some more holiday reading, try *A Turkey for Thanksgiving* by Eve Bunting (Clarion Books, 1995), which tells the story of a group of animal friends in search of a turkey to complete their Thanksgiving celebration—as a guest of honor instead of on a plate!

🐾 Flip to Chapter 43, "School's Out!" for a list of great summer camps and day programs especially designed for kids who care about the animals and the earth.

🐾 To get spruced up for Arbor Day, go to the National Arbor Day Foundation Web site at www.arborday.org, or call toll free 1-888-448-7337. They'll help you with lots of information on national activities, as well as ideas to help you branch out celebrations into your local neighborhood.

CHAPTER 31

Dressing Cool to Be Kind

Fur is not the only clothing made at a huge cost to animals: their very lives! Leather, down, silk, and wool come from animals who didn't want to let it go, either.

Did You Know?

- Most leather is cow skin. Many people who kill animals for meat also run their own leather tanneries. Talk about greedy—factory farmers have said they make a profit from every part of the cow except the "moo."
- Lots of vegetarian celebrities, like actress Pamela Anderson, demand animal-free wardrobes on their film sets. Actor Joaquin Phoenix, who starred in the movie *Walk the Line,* insisted that his costumes be cruelty free from head to toe—even his hat and cowboy boots were made of fake leather and approved by PETA.

THEY SAID IT!

Here's what some celebs have to say about dressing cool, not cruel:

"It is the twenty-first century. I don't think that we should use the flesh or the skin of any creature to make ourselves look good. The abuse that is involved in Australian wool is so outrageous to me. We can do something that's really compassionate or something that's cruel. I really make every effort in my life to make the compassionate choice."
—Alicia Silverstone

"I try not to wear animal products like leather and stuff."
—Andy Hurley, Fall Out Boy

"With MADE we don't want any part of contributing to any kind of animal cruelty. We want to do what we can to encourage people to get products that don't encourage animal cruelty. We're just really happy to be able to have a clothing company and to be able to make that decision [not to use leather]. It feels good when you go to sleep at night, like 'Wow, you know, I was nice. I was good to the world today.' That's a good feeling; it's rewarding."
—Benji Madden of Good Charlotte on their clothing company, MADE

🐾 To turn animal skins into leather, tanners use substances such as formaldehyde that are harmful to us and to the environment. These substances give leather its funny smell. Leather also comes from horses, pigs, and lambs who are killed for food. But some animals, including mules, turtles, snakes, zebras, and kangaroos, are killed just for their skin! When you see a leather handbag, belt, or pair of cowboy boots made of these kinds of skins, please tell the wearer that up to a third of "exotic" leathers come from illegally killed endangered animals.

- Vegan champion skater Ed Templeton has been designing leather-free skate shoes since the early nineties, using all sorts of really cool cruelty-free materials. He has two popular signature pro skate shoe models available from the company Emerica, and they are 100 percent synthetic. You can check them out at www.emericaskate.com.

- Don't be a woolly bully! Wool is the sheared coat of a sheep. If you get cold in the winter without your coat, imagine how shaved (or shorn) sheep feel—sheep whose wool has gone to market feel the cold even more than we humans do when we're naked!

- Sheep breeders have created a special type of sheep called merinos, who produce huge amounts of wool because their skin is very wrinkled. This overload of wool causes millions of them to pass out in the heat every summer. The extra wrinkles also cause another problem: maggots get into the wool. So to prevent maggots from getting a toehold, the sheep breeders actually cut away the flesh around and under the lamb's tail. This is called *mulesing*. It is extremely painful and takes a very long time to heal.

- Silk comes from the shiny fiber that silkworms weave for their cocoons. To take the silk from the silkworm, the silkworms are boiled or steamed alive in their cocoons! If someone asks "Who cares?" just answer "The silkworms do, so I do too!"

🐾 Down is the insulating feather coat of ducks and geese. Down feathers come from birds who have been killed (to make pâté, for example) or are plucked (pulled) from living animals' bodies—not just once, but, in some countries, four or five times during their lives. Pulling out their feathers hurts at least as much as it hurts to pull out an eyebrow hair, but all over your whole body. Down is *so* out!

What You Can Do

🐾 The Flintstones may have had to wear animal-based clothing, but there's no excuse now for dressing like a caveman or cavewoman! Smart fashions are kind to animals. Choose clothing made from plant-based fibers such as cotton, canvas, and linen and from synthetic (human-made) materials such as acrylic, rayon, and polyester.

🐾 Check wallets, belts, watchbands, soccer balls, and any other products so you can avoid those made of leather. Instead, choose nylon wallets, metal or plastic watchbands, plastic or cotton belts, and vinyl balls. If you get a gift made of wool, down, silk, or leather, you might consider asking the gift giver to exchange it for something not made from animals.

🐾 Try synthetic running shoes from Nike, New Balance, or Adidas, or all-purpose shoes from Converse, Diesel, Target, Vans, Etnies, Steve Madden, Alloy, Moo Shoes, Otsu, Food Fight, MADE, Level 27, Atticus, Visions Streetware, Paul Frank, American Apparel, Wal-Mart or Kmart. When you're shopping, if you can't smell the difference (leather is very smelly!) ask the salesperson for help. If you're not sure what's made of what, look for the words "man-made materials," "synthetic," or "non-leather" on the shoe.

🐾 Instead of down, follow the lead of most mountain climbers and choose a coat made of Polyguard or Thinsulate. These synthetic materials keep you warmer and drier than down. If you have a down comforter, pillow, and other feathery items, when they wear out, replace them with something that won't bring you (or the birds) down.

🐾 Advertise! Display your taste for cruelty-free clothes by getting badges and patches for your fake fur and leather that shout out: FAKE—NOT LEATHER and FAUX—NOT FUR. You can order these from PETA. Call 757-622-PETA or go to www.petamall.com.

Check It Out

🐾 PETA has a lot of great Web sites for finding out about how important it is to let animals keep their skins—and the cool alternatives available to all of us when we shop. Log on to www.cowsarecool.com, www.shedyourskin.com, and www.savethesheep.com to become the local expert on the issues!

🐾 For a good selection of "pleather," synthetic, and fabric shoes, visit a Payless Shoe Store or write for catalogs to:

- Aesop Unlimited, P.O. Box 315, N. Cambridge, MA 02140, or call 617-628-8030. Visit www.aesopinc.com, or e-mail aesop@aesopinc.com.

- Heartland Products (www.trvnet.net/~hrtlndp), who carry shoes, jackets, and baseball/softball gloves made without leather. They feature several products from the U.K.'s Vegetarian Shoes, as well as vegan Birkenstocks and cowboy boots. Write to Box 218, Dakota City, IA 50529, or call 1-800-441-4692.

- "Pleather" (plastic leather) softballs, in white and fluorescent colors, are available from Spalding. Call them for free at 1-800-SPALDING for more information or visit www.spalding.com. They also produce vegan volleyballs, basketballs, soccer balls, and footballs.

- To find the store nearest you that sells Nike non-leather sneakers, call 1-800-344-NIKE, visit www.nike.com, or write to Nike USA Consumer Services, P.O. Box 4027, Beaverton, OR 97076-4027.

Patagonia makes a lot of attractive, warm, non-animal active-wear clothes, including a non-chinchilla "synchilla" jacket! Call to ask for the latest catalog at 1-800-638-6464, visit www.patagonia.com, or write to Patagonia Mail Order, P.O. Box 32050, Reno, NV 89523-2050.

32

Pig Out!

Sick of the same old "meat and potatoes"? Do you know why vegans have such fun with food? Take a quick quiz and get wise on cruelty-free surprises:

1. Which of the following can be made without animal ingredients?
   a. Thanksgiving turkey roast
   b. Chicken schnitzel
   c. Cheesecake

2. A vegan pizza is topped with:
   a. Nothing—it is just dough with tomato sauce
   b. Mozzarella, pepperoni, barbecue sauce, and crispy chicken
   c. Bean shoots and tofu

3. If you're a vegan at a barbecue, you'll be able to eat:
    a. Only the salads
    b. Chunky burgers and barbecue ribs
    c. Just dry bread rolls

4. Vegan food equals:
    a. None of the yummy foods like ice cream, hot dogs, and chocolate or cakes
    b. Lettuce, bean sprouts, and tofu
    c. Healthier versions of every delicious food you can think of!

Answers: 1. a, b, *and* c! All of them have mock meat equivalents!; 2. b: All these ingredients have vegan alternatives too! 3. b: You can enjoy delicious vegan barbecues—just take along your own veggie burgers and soy "riblets." 4. c: There are vegan alternatives for almost everything that contains animal ingredients—without the harmful animal fats and hormones. Check the vegan product list at the back of this book to see what's out there.

Did You Know?

🐾 Veggie burgers, dogs, and nuggets are made from soy beans or wheat. Soybeans can be processed and shaped into all kinds of foods that look and taste just like the things lots of new vegetarians might miss. Hot dogs, hamburgers, cold cuts, ice cream, milk, and any thing else you can imagine can be

made out of soybeans or other beans, grains, or vegetables. Some of them are better than others, but there's so much variety. Check out our favorites in Appendix B in the back of this book.

- Professional BMX rider Aaron Behnke has been a vegetarian for more than 10 years, *and* he makes sure he keeps all his gear cow friendly by accepting sponsorship only from companies that have quality vegan and leather-free products, like UGP and Etnies.

- Lots of ballparks now offer vegetarian hot dogs and yummy veggie burgers. Some of these are McAfee Coliseum (Oakland), Coors Field (Colorado), Rogers Centre (Toronto), Citizens Bank Park (Philadelphia), Tropicana Field (Tampa Bay), Miller Park (Milwaukee), Bank One Ballpark (Arizona), Dolphins Stadium (Florida), and PNC Park (Pittsburgh). The San Francisco Giants' SBC Park even offers vegetarian sushi rolls, mushroom sandwiches, and *edamame*, a Japanese snack made from salted soy—hey, those nutritious beans just never stop working!

🐾 Benji Madden and Billy Martin of the band Good Charlotte are big animal protectors and total vegans. When on the road they chow down on all their favorites, like Tofutti frozen pizzas, Boca Burgers, Starbucks' Soy Lattes, Gardenburger Riblets, waffles, waffles, and—that's right, you guessed it— more waffles, with soy ice cream and syrup, their fave breakfast feast.

🐾 Pigs are very smart and clean animals (if someone doesn't round them up and stick them in a filthy pen!) who can communicate with us even more effectively than dogs can. Pigs cared for by people who enjoy their company (and not the way they taste!) learn to understand many human words, become housebroken, and show much affection to their human rescuers. Pigs are very happy animals when not bullied or kept in tiny stalls on factory farms.

🐾 Cows and bulls are natural vegetarians. On factory farms their babies are taken away from them after only a day or two. These calves are not allowed to enjoy the outdoors, and they're shipped in dark, crowded trucks to be killed to make hamburgers or "all-beef franks."

🐾 Turkeys raised for lunch meat and turkey franks have a terrible time on today's factory farms, too. They are kept in such cramped conditions that farmers cut their beaks and toes off so they don't hurt each other out of frustration. They are bred to have such big bodies that their legs can give way under all that weight.

What You Can Do

🐾 You can save pigs, cows, and turkeys by eating veggie dogs instead of hot dogs. There are some great tasting veggie dogs made by a company called Yves. Every grocery store now carries veggie dogs, so you can bring them to cookouts and share them with everyone. For lunch, pack a faux meat sandwich made with Fakin' Bacon, Phoney Baloney, or Smoky Tofurky! You can find fake meats in most grocery stores now.

🐾 Morningstar Farms and Boca make amazing vegan veggie burgers as well as Chik'n Nuggets and Steak Strips, which are great for adding to salads and stir-fries. To find out where you can buy Morningstar Farms products go to the Web site Store-Finder (www.kelloggs.com/brand/msfarms/) and www .vegcooking.com. The site also has great veg recipe ideas for cooking with these products!

🐾 If you're missing the flavor of a grill or barbecue, Garden-burger makes a delicious Meatless Flame Grilled Chicken as well as Meatless BBQ Chicken, Sweet and Sour Pork, and Meatless Riblets made out of soy and wheat gluten, which are delicious hot and smothered in barbecue sauce! See www.gardenburger.com for where to buy them and lots more cooking ideas.

🐾 Your grocery store probably stocks some faux meats, but if not, ask to meet with the manager of your local store to ask her or him to carry these products. Ask your friends to fill out comment cards, too. Make copies of the list of some good vegetarian foods (visit www.vegcooking.com for suggestions) and give a copy to all the local grocery store managers. If you have a Whole Foods, Wild Oats, or Trader Joe's in your town, you'll find a gold mine of veggie options in their freezer cases.

🐾 Everyone knows slaughterhouses are ugly places, but since many people can't imagine not eating animals, they don't want to think about what happened to their dinner when it was still an animal. Learn how animals are raised on factory farms, how they are transported, and how they are killed. The facts aren't pretty, but knowing them will help you stick up for the animals and stick to your new diet.

🐾 Don't be a meat addict! Eat for life: your own life and the an-imals' lives (since meat is high in fat and cholesterol, it is un-healthy as well as cruel).

Can You Believe It?

Read up on these gross-out facts that will have you gagging:

🐾 Today's poultry slaughterhouses are so disgusting, one former U.S. Department of Agriculture scientist says that the "final product is no different than if you stuck it in the toilet and ate it." If you haven't been turned off at the idea of eating animals already, here are some more totally "out there" accounts of what you're risking when meat is on the menu—get the sick bag ready, because these filthy facts might just bring up dinner!

🐾 Government inspectors recently discovered that students in 31 states were served chicken nuggets made from birds covered with pus, bruises, tumors, or scabs. Wait—it gets worse! The inspectors said that factory-farmed chickens commonly suffer from infections that cause pockets of pus to form in parts of their bodies. The pus-coated bird bits go into a mixture called a "binder," which is used in chicken nuggets and patties.

🐾 A family in Virginia uncovered a foul find in their box of chicken wings: a fried chicken's head with the beak and eyes intact! But, hey, according to the local health inspector, there's nothing wrong with eating fried chicken heads. "Even the beak will simply crunch apart in your mouth." Yuck!

🐾 Another family, in Canada, received an unusual topping on their daughter's burger: a rat's severed head—complete with eyes, teeth, nose, and whiskers.

🐾 A fast-food customer in the United Kingdom got a stomach-turning surprise when she found a caterpillar crawling around on her chicken sandwich, and back in the States, a family was chowing down on a bucket of chicken parts when one of the daughters asked, "Mommy, what's that crawling out of your mouth?" Answer: a maggot! After checking out the rest of the bucket, the family discovered maggots crawling all over it. Meat is *dead,* that's for sure!

Check It Out

- Just have a look at the fantastic list of vegan meat alternatives in Appendix B at the back of this book and you're guaranteed to salivate. Take it to the supermarket when you go shopping and suggest to your parents that they buy some of the products. If you can't find any, suggest to the store that they begin stocking them!

- If you just can't get enough information on vegetarianism, tasty vegan foods, and, most importantly, the animals, you cannot go past PETA's www.vegkids.com site, where you will find everything from facts, recipes, stickers, celebrities, and ideas for activism to a whole lot of related links. You can also order your free Vegetarian Starter Kit and a free comic called *A Cow's Life!*

CHAPTER 33

Too Hot for Spot!
In hot weather, leave dogs at home.
HelpingAnimals.com **PeTA**

Take Care of Hot Dogs

Do you know a dog who wears a coat and pants? You probably do, so help keep him or her from getting hot under the collar too! In the summer, the temperature inside a car can get hot enough to fry an egg, but a dog in a hot car is no "yoke."

Did You Know?

- When the temperature is above 70°F, the inside of a parked ear can reach 120° to 175°F within minutes—*even with the windows cracked.*
- Even in the shade, a hot car can quickly become an oven.
- Even if the car air-conditioning was on until you left the car, hot air swiftly replaces the cold.
- Animals left in cars can suffer serious, sometimes fatal, heatstroke.
- Dogs "sweat" only through their footpads and through their mouths, by panting.

What You Can Do

🐾 Never leave an animal in a parked car in warm weather, even for a few minutes.

🐾 Watch for animals left in cars in parking lots on hot days. If you see one, immediately call the police, humane society, or animal control. Ask for help freeing the animal if she or he is panting heavily or collapsing.

🐾 If the car is outside a large store, ask the manager to make an announcement over the loudspeaker. Lots of lucky dogs have been saved this way!

🐾 Pour cold water from a nearby business or public rest room over an animal to lower his or her temperature and hopefully save his or her life.

🐾 Call radio stations and ask them to make "Hot Dog Warning" public service announcements.

🐾 Show shopping-mall managers the facts on your flyers, and ask them to have stores in the mall set out PLEASE TAKE ONE holders for your flyers. You can offer to supply the holders. Clean half-gallon beverage cartons decorated with contact paper, with the top and front cut out, are easy and fun to make.

🐾 Ask mall managers to announce over the PA system several times a day that animal protection agencies will break a window or door lock, if necessary, to get an animal out of a car.

🐾 Dogs aren't the only ones who need to chill out in the summer. Other animals like birds and rabbits in cages might need your help to cool off, too. Look out for dogs on chains and rabbits in hutches who might not be getting fresh water daily. Remind the owners politely to fill the animals' water and make sure they keep it up. You can easily turn a shallow baking pan into a birdbath for your feathered friends to frolic in on hot days—just make sure you change the water every day to keep it nice and clean for them.

HE DID IT!

Isiah Ayala knows that summer can be deadly for dogs locked in hot cars even with the windows rolled down. When he was nine years old he found two pups panting in a parked car in 90-degree weather. Luckily he was prepared and he managed to aim his Super Soaker water gun through the cracked window and kept them cool with the water until animal control officers arrived to rescue the dogs. For keeping the lucky pups alive, Isiah was recognized as a hero by Santa Cruz County Animal Control and the Doris Day Animal League.

Check It Out

🐾 Make a flyer to inform people of the dangers of leaving their dogs unattended in the car and put them on windshields in shopping centers and around the neighborhood during warm weather. You can find information for making your flyer on PETA's Web site www.helpinganimals.com and from your local animal shelter. You can also order copies of PETA's brochure *Don't Let Your Dog Get Hot Under the Collar* from www.petaliterature.com.

CHAPTER 34

Oh, Deer!

Wouldn't it be awful, wouldn't it be queer,
To be playing in the woods and be shot by a deer?
To be strolling with friends in the afternoon sun,
Just to be stopped by some deer with a gun,
And blasted to bits while out having some fun?
So consider this thought and remember it clear,
It wouldn't be fun to be shot by a deer.

—Pete Traynor

Some people chase and kill animals like quail, pheasants, rabbits, and deer and call it "sport," but isn't sport an activity that involves people who choose to play the game and can call "time out" if they don't?

One fall, a Michigan deer hunter came upon a buck and doe standing side by side in the forest. It was strange, but they did not run from him, so the hunter raised his rifle and killed the buck. Despite the loud gunshot, the doe still didn't move. The hunter walked right up to her. It was then that he realized she was completely blind. Looking closely at the buck, he noticed that there was an area of fur worn away from his *left* side, matching the bare patch on the doe's *right* side. The hunter realized that, by pressing his side against hers, the buck had led the blind doe through the forest and cared for her, staying beside her, rather than running from the hunter and saving his own life. Who ever thought that animals don't have friends and feelings like we do?

Did You Know?

- Every year, hunters in the United States kill more than 200 million animals, not to mention quite a few people who are killed or wounded when shot by mistake. That is more than twice as many animals being shot as there are people in the whole state of California (24 million), New York (18 million), Illinois (11 million), Michigan (9 million), Ohio (11 million), Pennsylvania (12 million), and Texas (15 million) all put together!
- Many hunters use "calls" that mimic the real calls of animals in distress, then blast away when other animals come to the rescue.
- It's illegal to hunt a deer swimming in water above her knees in North Carolina and illegal to use a call to imitate an animal in Miami! Don't you wish every state enforced those and even tougher laws?
- Some hunters say that if they don't kill animals in the fall, the animals will starve in winter, yet animals were here long before humans were, and they did just fine, thank you very much, without being hunted. In fact, in places where hunting is legal, animal populations actually grow every year because "game" agencies make sure animals are fooled into having more young, which they do when they think there's enough food for a big family. Also, hunters usually try to shoot big, healthy animals—the ones who have the best chance at making it through the winter—not the sick or frail.

🐾 Only 7 percent of Americans hunt. The majority of people in the United States enjoy seeing free-roaming animals alive and kickin'.

🐾 In Arizona, it is illegal to shoot or hunt camels. Isn't that weird? Well, catch this: In Kansas City it is illegal to hunt whales, and in Kentucky it is illegal to shoot animals out of the window of a moving vehicle, with the *exception* of a whale!

🐾 In November 2004 the British government voted to outlaw foxhunting, a country "sport" in which foxes are chased and eventually torn to bits by dogs. The ban was introduced after many years of protests by animal rights groups and Hunt Saboteurs, people who lure the hounds away from the chase by blowing horns in the wrong direction, by putting smelly rags around that hide the smell of the fox, and generally getting in the hunters' way. The U.K. victory shows that it pays to protest and never give up!

🐾 Some people who want animals to live unharmed try to disrupt hunts by putting human hair from barber shops (or even lions' dung from the zoo) around trees where hunters build platforms. The smell alerts animals to the presence of the enemy.

🐾 Creepy-crawlies in Ohio are lucky: it's against the law to kill a housefly within 160 feet of a church without a license, and in Cleveland it's illegal to catch mice without a hunting license. What other laws would you like to see enacted?

What You Can Do

Here are some ideas to help the animals who live in the woods near you:

🐾 If you live in the country, make big signs that say NO HUNTING and hang them on trees and fences all over your property. Get your friends to do the same.

🐾 Some plots of land have been set aside for animals. These are called wildlife refuges and were meant to be safe places for animals to live in. While people can't build houses on the refuges, some refuges allow people to hunt on them. Write to your congressperson to protest hunting on national wildlife refuges (you can find out who your congressperson is at your local library or do a quick search on the Internet). Send your letter to the House of Representatives, Washington, DC 20515, or to the United States Senate, Washington, DC 20510. Your letter can be short and sharp, like the following:

> Dear Senator [name],
>
> What good are national wildlife refuges to the animals? People hunt and trap there. It is a shame because the animals have no place to be safe. Please make our national wildlife refuges the safe places they were meant to be by making hunting and trapping in them illegal.
>
> Sincerely,
> [Your name]

🐾 Contact the U.S. Fish and Wildlife Service for information on exactly where national wildlife refuges are. You can find the agency at www.fws.gov, by calling 1-800-344-WILD, or by writing to U.S. Fish and Wildlife Service 1849 C St. NW, Washington, DC 20242.

🐾 If people in your family hunt, try to persuade them to carry a camera rather than a gun into the woods. Animals "shot" with a camera can still go home at night to take care of their babies. That's as long as they're not in Alaska, where, even though it is legal to hunt a bear, it is illegal to wake a bear up to take a photo!

Check It Out

🐾 Visit the Fund for Animals Web site at www.marylandbears .com to learn how to protest bear hunts. You can also call them at 1-888-405-FUND.

🐾 For more information and a fact sheet called *Why Sport Hunting Is Cruel and Unnecessary* visit PETA's www.helpinganimals .com site and www.peta.org, or call or write to PETA at 501 Front St., Norfolk, VA 23510, phone 757-622-PETA.

CHAPTER 35

Give a Well-Come Gift

If anyone calls you a drip,
Say, "a drip is a drop,
A drop is water,
Water is nature,
And nature is beautiful!"
—Karen Pratt, age eight

To get a drink of clean water, most people just turn on a tap. Imagine if there was no running water and you didn't live near a river! That's what it's like for many little animals who live in the city and can't turn on the water faucets themselves.

If you watch birds after a good rain, you can see them drinking little raindrops off the tips of leaves, but what do they do when it hasn't rained for a while?

Since birds and other beings who live in the city must work hard and think hard how to survive, they seek out any little puddles of water they can find. Cracks and dips in the pavement can hold water after it has rained, but look at the water: it can be shiny with motor oil or full of trash. Drinking it could be hazardous to anyone's health, but sometimes animals have no choice.

Did You Know?

- Animal bodies, including yours, are 98 percent water!
- A camel can drink up to thirty gallons of water at one time!
- The only rodent who doesn't drink water is a kind of desert rat called the kangaroo rat. Kangaroo rats get all the water they need by eating the juicy leaves of desert plants. Another desert rat rolls a stone in front of her burrow every night to catch the dew so that she can drink in the morning.
- One type of desert frog can wait as long as seven years for water by surrounding himself in a type of see-through bag that becomes his first meal once the rain comes.
- Once evaporated, a water molecule spends about 10 days in the air as mist.

What You Can Do

Turn on the tap for those who can't:

- Turn a shallow baking pan into a birdbath to allow feathered beings to splash around and cool down on hot days. Hint: Water pans must always be kept clean and should never be more than two inches deep, or birds, especially youngsters, can slip in and not be able to get out again. Change the water every day.
- Clean out trash from watering holes in the pavement or in other places where birds and other animals may drink.
- Trees need water, too. A healthy tree is a living home for lots of animals. Dump a pan of water at the base of a tree "house" in hot weather, turn on the garden hose and/or sprinkler for

plants and trees. The evening or early morning is the best time or you can scorch the plants.

🐾 Look out for dogs on chains and rabbits in hutches; they need water bowls with fresh water daily. Ask your neighbors to let you secure water bowls in tires or onto a fence to avoid spills, or weigh the bowls down with clean rocks or a brick. Scrub out and refill water bowls at home, too.

🐾 For little animals like hamsters, mice, and guinea pigs who use bottles, make sure their water bottles are clean and their necks unclogged. And leave a little bowl of water, too, for safety's sake, because it would be absolutely terrible if you thought they were able to drink but the bottle wasn't working!

Check It Out

🐾 For more ideas, write to PETA (501 Front St., Norfolk, VA 23510), or log on to www.petakids.com.

🐾 Find out more about animals who may be in danger during hot weather. Read Chapter 33, "Take Care of Hot Dogs," for the details on saving hot dogs!

🐾 Point your mouse to Pond Dip (http://web.ukonline.co.uk/conker/pond-dip/). Pond Dip is a Web site created for kids by kids who have a wildlife pond in their garden or would like a pond. You can join in and post reports and pictures of the wildlife you have seen in your pond. If you haven't a pond, there's even a page about how you can easily make one.

CHAPTER 36

Critter Chatter

Words we say, hear, and read have a powerful effect on us and how we see others. Sometimes people develop bad feelings about animals simply from the words they choose.

Did You Know

- 🐾 It's silly to insult people by calling them names like "pig" or "goose," when pigs are really very smart and friendly (in ancient times they were considered sacred), and geese love their families and protect them, even in the face of grave personal danger.
- 🐾 Pigs don't "eat like pigs." They are not sloppy eaters; they chew slowly and move their food around with their snouts to fully release its aroma so that they can really enjoy it. The only time pigs overeat is when their food contains drugs that factory farmers use to fatten them faster.

🐾 Making animals out to be mean, or timid, or dirty or selfish helps people feel better about treating them cruelly or using them for their own wants without thinking about what the animals' true nature and real needs may be. We have to shake off that way of thinking.

What You Can Do

🐾 In school or at a party or get-together, see who can write down the most names of animals that people use to insult each other. Then write down those animals' good points beside their names. Next, pledge to stop using names of animals as insults and to use them as compliments instead, e.g. "Your memory is as good as an elephant's!"

🐾 What's wrong with this sentence? "The dog was hungry, so I fed it." If you're tuned in to how language is misused when animals are involved, you'll show your respect for animals by calling them "he" or "she," "some*one*" (not "some*thing*"), and never "it." "It" refers to things like a table, not living beings. If you're not sure, just say "she or he" or "he or she." Avoid saying "which" or "that" when referring to an animal. For example, "Do you think the crow *who* slid down the window on his bottom for fun is the very same crow we saw riding the air current, over and over again, just for fun?"

🐾 Avoid ugly expressions like "kill two birds with one stone," "wear kid gloves," or "make a silk purse out of a sow's ear." Get out of the habit by making a beeper noise whenever you catch yourself or a friend saying negative things about animals.

🐾 Instead of "pet," say "friend," "companion," or "companimal," and say "friend," "companion," or "protector" instead of "owner" or "master." Animals aren't our property, they are not our slaves—they're our friends, or at least they should be.

🐾 Write to the editor of your local newspaper and ask that the paper adopt a policy of referring to animals as "he" or "she" (or "s/he," which you can write but can't pronounce), not "it."

- Ask your teacher please to have the class refer to animals as individuals, not objects, and to describe other-than-human beings in positive ways. Suggest a class discussion about referring to animals properly, so that others will realize the need to show them respect.

- Stop fooling yourself by calling the flesh of dead animals "meat," "veal," "pork," or "poultry." Start saying "cows," "calves," "pigs," "chickens," and "turkeys." Remembering where these "foods" came from makes us think about what—or whom—is being eaten.

- If you hear someone say, "He acted like an animal," remind that person that it's usually *humans* who wage wars, steal, cheat, and act spitefully toward each other. And anyway, we human beings are just another type of animal—that's a biological fact!

Check It Out

- Spend time reading a magazine or newspaper and underline words that refer to an animal as "it" or "which." Also mark places where writers refer to animals to describe things humans do, and any article that says cruelties like hunting or wearing fur are cool. It may shock you to realize how often all this happens!

- Go to www.sharetheworld.com and download some of their Just Choices activity sheets, which will give you exciting ways to become more aware of how to read and write the *right* way with respect for all living beings.

CHAPTER 37

Pack a Lunch with Punch

Can you imagine being locked in a classroom in semi-darkness, unable to move from your desk, turn around, or even go to the rest room—for months on end!
Now you've an idea what factory farms are like.

—School Campaign for Reaction Against Meat brochure
(The Vegetarian Society of the U.K.)

Lunchtime is a great time to promote kindness to animals. After all, we make life-and-death decisions for animals (and ourselves) at the lunch counter every day. Let your friends and classmates know that they can vote yes to life by "eating veggie" for lunch.

Did You Know?

🐾 Lunches offered at most schools today are full of grease, or animal fat, which is very bad for us. Purely vegetarian foods are much lower in fat than animal foods and don't have any cholesterol in them at all.

🐾 Twenty percent of young Americans have high cholesterol levels, and kids as young as six are developing clogged arteries, which can cause heart attacks and other health problems later on in life. High cholesterol can be caused by eating too much fat and too many animal products like meat, eggs, and dairy products.

🐾 Hunzas, people who live in the Himalayan mountains in Pakistan, eat almost no animal products. Most of these people live to be at least 100 years old, dancing and singing on their one-hundredth birthdays.

🐾 Because so many dolphins have been killed in drift nets set out to catch tuna, students in Milford, Connecticut, and Aurora, Colorado, got their schools to take tuna off their lunch menus. By talking to your principal or food service director, circulating a petition, or holding an assembly about how animals are raised for food, your group can try to get veal taken off—and tofu added to—your school's menu.

🐾 Paul McCartney, who was in the Beatles rock band and whom many consider to be the most successful musician ever, brings a vegetarian chef with him on tour. No meat is allowed backstage at the concerts, and anyone caught eating it there is thrown out!

🐾 Anyone who participates in the massive Vans Warped Tour (including bands, tabling crews, and roadies) are asked to nominate their food preference for catering from three choices of vegan, vegetarian, or meat eater every year. Vegan is the most popular choice!

What You Can Do

Since you probably can't take a vegetarian chef with you to school every day, work to get more (and more tasty) meatless dishes and meals served in your lunchroom. After all, you can't live on green beans alone! There are lots of easy-to-make foods such as veggie burgers, veggie dogs, nuggets, and vegetarian chili.

- 🐾 Let the cooks in the cafeteria know your many reasons for not wanting to eat meat. Encourage other kids to speak to them, too.
- 🐾 If you have difficulty getting your school to agree to serve vegetarian meals and options, ask your parents to speak to the principal.
- 🐾 While you're campaigning for healthy meals at school, you may want to "brown-bag it." Peanut butter and jelly on whole-grain bread, falafel or soy "meat" sandwiches, fruit salad, and trail mix are just a few of the healthy foods you can take to school for lunch.

Check It Out

- 🐾 Check out the list of vegan foods and ready-made meals in Appendix B at the back of this book and suggest to your teacher that you have some classes where you are taught about vegetarian foods and how to make meals with meat substitutes.
- 🐾 Write to the Physicians Committee for Responsible Medicine (PCRM), for their complete plan for healthy cafeteria lunches. This group of doctors and health experts will be happy to help you work with your school. You can find out more at www.pcrm.org, by writing to 5100 Wisconsin Ave. NW, Suite 400, Washington, DC 20016, or by e-mailing them at pcrm@pcrm.org.

SHE DID IT!

When Shakira Croce was just 14 years old, she vegetarianized her school cafeteria. She has also started her own animal rights group called Students Promoting Awareness of Animal Rights. You can check out their Web site at www.geocities .com/spaarclub/SPAAR.html. Here's what she says:

"Our head lunchroom lady did not think that enough students would eat their veggies instead of the daily 'mystery meat,' so at first she refused to provide a salad bar for the students. I circulated a petition among my fellow students to prove her wrong. Most kids (even non-vegetarians) wanted more options at our cafeteria—especially a fresh salad bar. In less than one week I had accumulated over 200 signatures. When I presented my petition to the lunch lady, she finally agreed to make a salad bar available for students."

You can vegetarianize your cafeteria too! Here are some helpful tips:

1. Be polite, but firm: When dealing with adults who have ideas that differ from yours, always have a smile on your face and speak in a nice tone of voice.
2. Everyone's signature counts! Approach everyone, including teachers. This is a great way to meet new people and make new friends.
3. Be informative: Take this as an opportunity to inform others of the benefits of vegetarianism. If people don't want to sign the petition at first, give them some information to tell them why they should.

You are old enough to make choices based on what you believe is right and wrong. If equal opportunity is not given to those of us who are vegetarians, you must do something to bring about change!

- Check out the Vegetarian Society Youth Pages at www.vegsoc .org/youth/, which have links to vegetarian guides for nursery, school, and college caterers as well as recipe ideas for young people.
- Log onto www.petacatalog.com and order your own lunch bag bearing the message NO ANIMALS IN HERE or a bright yellow satchel that features a cute baby chicken shouting out "I am not a nugget." While you're there, follow the link to www.vegcooking.com and www.vegetarianstarterkit.com, where you'll find enough information and yummy recipes to share around with all your friends at recess.
- If you want more facts to show people that vegetarianism is a healthy diet, you'll find all the information you need at www.foodstudies.org and www.choiceusa.net, two sites promoting vegetarian cafeterias and listing all the reasons vegetarians are some of the healthiest kids around!

CHAPTER 38

Be a Bookworm

Question: Why didn't the burglar break into the library?
Answer: Because he was afraid he'd get a long sentence!

Like animals, books are wonderful companions. They let a chicken tell us why she likes to scratch in the dirt or a dog explain the relief of having a thorn pulled out of his paw. This chapter lists some terrific books about animals and our relationships with them. Your school or local library probably has some of them already; ask your teacher or librarian to help you get the others. Maybe you can get a copy of your own for your birthday or save up to buy one for yourself!

Did You Know?

🐾 There are over 50,000 books published each year in the United States.

🐾 Books used to be chained to the bookshelves in libraries—
let's try to make the chaining of animals in circuses and zoos
history too!

You can learn all these things and more from reading books:

🐾 Humans aren't the only ones to use tools. Sea otters use
stones as hammers and open up shells with them.

🐾 Finches on the Galapagos Islands use a cactus spine or a
sharp twig as a fork!

🐾 Chimpanzees sometimes crumple leaves to make a sponge
so they can get drinking water trapped in places they otherwise couldn't reach.

🐾 The male regent bowerbird paints with a brush and natural colors. Mixing saliva with earth color, plant pigments, and char-
coal, he dips a piece of bark or a wadded leaf into the "paint"
and creates green or blue-gray murals in his living space.

🐾 Honeybees dance to communicate with their sisters. Like us,
they speak in symbols. For example, when a forager bee returns to the hive to tell her sisters that she has found a good
place to get nectar and pollen, she runs around in a figure
eight. The other bees can tell how far away the place is by
how long she runs. In one species of honeybee, running for
one second means the nectar is five kilometers from the hive,
and a two-second run means they'll only have to go two kilometers from the hive.

What You Can Do

🐾 Look in your library and bookstores for books that tell more
about the special characteristics and behaviors of animals,
such as *My Life with the Chimpanzees*, by Jane Goodall
(Pocket/Minstrel, 1988, ages 8–16).

🐾 Some great books about animal rights are also available in your local library. In nonfiction, try: *Pets Without Homes* by Caroline Arnold (for preschoolers), *Animal Experimentation: Cruelty or Science* by Nancy Day (for older teens); and *Animals Have Rights Too* by Michael W. Fox (for teens) or *Who Cares About Animal Rights* by Michael Twinn (One World, 1992, ages 6–16).

In fiction you can read: *Who Will Speak for the Lamb* by Mildred Ames, about an animal rights issue in high school (for teens); and *Grusha* by Barbara Falk, about a bear's unhappiness in a circus (for preschoolers).

Check 'Em Out!

Classics

- 🐾 *Beautiful Joe,* Marshall Saunders, retold by Quinn Currie (Storytellers Ink, 1990). First written in 1893, this is the remarkable true story of a rescued dog born in a stable on the outskirts of a small town in Maine.
- 🐾 *Black Beauty,* Anna Sewell (first published in 1877; new edition by Storytellers Ink, 1998). A horse is passed from "owner" to "owner," encountering both the good and the bad of humanity.
- 🐾 *Blueberries for Sal,* Robert McCloskey (The Viking Press, 1976). The sweet story of a little girl and a bear cub who mistakenly begin to follow each other's mothers while out picking blueberries (for preschoolers).
- 🐾 *Charlotte's Web,* E. B. White (Harper, Row and Dell, 1952). Charlotte the spider and farm girl Fern work together to save Wilbur the pig from slaughter.
- 🐾 *Frederick,* Leo Lionni (Pantheon, 1967). While the rest of his mouse family is busy gathering traditional supplies to get them through the winter, Frederick tells them he is gathering things like sunshine and the colors of the meadows (for preschoolers).

🐾 *Lassie Come Home*, Eric Knight (Harmony, Raine and Co, 1981). First published in 1940, this is the touching story of a collie's love for her human friend.

🐾 *Make Way for Ducklings*, Robert McCloskey (Viking, 1941). The true story of how traffic was stopped in Boston, Massachusetts, to let a mother duck and her babies cross the street (for kids aged 4–8).

🐾 *My Friend Flicka*, Mary O'Hara (Harper & Row, 1943). A boy gains maturity through caring for a young horse.

🐾 *The Yearling*, Marjorie Rawlings (Charles Scribner's Sons, 1938; new edition by Collier Books). A boy adopts a baby deer, and the deer causes trouble for his family.

🐾 *The Red Pony*, John Steinbeck (Penguin, 1951). A coming-of-age novel about a boy and a pony.

🐾 *Stuart Little*, E. B. White (Harper & Row, 1945). The adventures of a mouse living with a family of humans.

Nonfiction

🐾 *Animals Have Rights Too*, Michael W. Fox (Continuum, 1991). A handbook for kids, parents, and teachers that explores how different ways of thinking and behaving can reduce all forms of animal suffering.

🐾 *Animals, Nature and Albert Schweitzer*, Ann Cottrell Free (The Flying Fox Press, 1988). A collection of writings by the Nobel Prize–winning doctor who proclaimed the ethic of reverence for all life.

🐾 *Born to Be Wild: The Livewire Guide to Saving Animals*, Juliet Gellatley (Livewire, 2000). A practical guide to animal rights action for young people.

🐾 *I Love Animals and Broccoli*, Debra Wasserman and Charles Stahler (Vegetarian Resource Group, P.O. Box 1463, Baltimore, MD 21203). A book of games, puzzles, and stories about healthy eating and caring about animals.

🐾 *Meeting Milo,* Yvette Van Veen (Perks, 2004). A fun book that will teach you how to play safely with dogs.

🐾 *What's the Big Idea: The Essential Guide to Animal Rights and Wrongs,* Anita Goneri (Hodder, 1997). A collection of facts and activities relating to animal rights issues.

🐾 *Zak: The One-of-a-Kind Dog,* Jane Lidz (Henry Abrams, 1997). A photographic essay about Zak and his many friends.

Fiction

🐾 *A Little Dog Like You,* Rosemary Sutcliffe (Simon and Schuster, 1990). The bittersweet story of Pippin, a tiny tan Chihuahua, and his life with a woman he calls Mommie.

🐾 *Every Living Thing,* Cynthia Rylant (Bradbury Press, 1985). Twelve stories about the extraordinary relationships between humans and other-than-human beings.

🐾 *Hey, Get Off Our Train,* John Burmingham (Dragonfly Books, 1989). The adventures of a little boy who goes on a train ride and finds endangered animal friends along the way (for ages 4–8).

🐾 *Martin's Mice,* Dick King-Smith (Crown Publishers Inc., 1989). A story about a companion cat who keeps mice as his own companion animals.

🐾 *Mrs. Frisby and the Rats of Nimh,* Robert C. O'Brien (Aladdin Fantasy, 1971). The story of a brave mouse who seeks help from the mysterious and wise rats living nearby.

🐾 *Much Ado About Aldo,* Johanna Hurwitz (Morrow, 1978). Because of a school project, 8-year-old Aldo stops eating meat.

🐾 *Nathan's Fishing Trip,* Lulu Delacre (Scholastic, Inc., 1988). A mouse and an elephant learn what a fishing trip means for the fishes (for preschoolers).

🐾 *One in a Million,* Nicholas Read (Raincoast Books, 1997). The story of a little stray pup, Joey, and his search for a loving family of human companions.

🐾 *Saving Emily*, Nicholas Reade (Prometheus, 2001). The story of a 12 year old boy who saves a heifer from a cattle auction.

🐾 *Saving Lilly*, Peg Kehret (Simon and Schuster, 2001). A novel about a group of children trying to save an elephant from the circus.

🐾 *The Best Cat in the World*, Leslea Newman (Eerdman's Books for Young Readers, 2004). Victor always told his cat Charlie that he was "the best cat in the world," and, when Charlie dies, Victor doesn't know how he can ever be replaced. Join him in his search for a new companion.

🐾 *The Bollo Caper*, Art Buchwald, illustrations by Elise Primavera (G. P. Putnam's Sons, 1983). Bollo, the most beautiful leopard in Africa, is trapped and brought to New York City to become a fur coat. He ends up in Washington, D.C., where he pushes along a bill to protect endangered species.

🐾 *The Great Pig Escape*, Linda Meller (O'Brien Press, 2000). A group of smart pigs escape from the confines of their farm.

🐾 *The Mare on the Hill*, Thomas Locker (Dial Books, 1985). A beautiful story about a mare who has previously been abused and the two children who patiently gain her trust.

🐾 *The Night Before Thanksgiving*, Natasha Wing (Reading Railroad Books, 2001). A group of kids liberate turkeys from a factory farm.

🐾 *Walter the Farting Dog*, William Kotzwinkle (Frog Ltd, 2001). The funny tale of a family who love Walter despite his incredible gas problem.

🐾 *Who Will Speak for the Lamb?*, Mildred Ames (Harper & Row Junior Books, 1989). With realistic characters, this story takes a stand for the rights of all other-than-human beings, especially those kept in laboratories.

🐾 *Victor the Vegetarian: Saving Little Lambs*, Radha Vignola (Avivia, 1994). When Victor overhears his father talk about killing the lambs on the farm so they can have lamb chops, he runs away with his lamb friends, Marigold and Buttercup.

True Stories/Autobiography

🐾 *A Chipmunk on My Shoulder*, G. J. Helbemal (Angus and Roberston, 1989). The author recounts experiences of sharing a London apartment with two chipmunks.

🐾 *Animal Angels: Amazing Acts of Love and Compassion*, Stephanie Laland (Conari Press, 1998). True stories about the courage, devotion, and kindness of animals.

🐾 *Arnie, the Darling Starling*, Margaret S. Corbo and Diane Marie Barras (Houghton Mifflin Co., 1983). A man cares for a starling who had fallen from his nest.

🐾 *Born Free: A Lioness of Two Worlds*, Joy Adamson (revised edition Pantheon 2000). Adamson recounts her adventures as the "mother" of an orphaned lion cub named Elsa.

🐾 *Friends of All Creatures*, Rose Evans (Sea Fog Press, 1984). A look at how people through the ages have shown compassion for animals.

🐾 *For the Love of Henry*, Dona K. Soler (Dorrence and Co, 1985). The true story of a friendly rooster named Henry.

🐾 *Kinship With All Life*, Allen Boone (Harper & Row, 1954). Real-life stories about communications between animals of different species, including between humans and other animals.

🐾 *My Life With the Chimpanzees*, Jane Goodall (Pocket Books, 1998). The famous primatologist describes her adventures in getting to know the chimpanzees of Gombe, Africa.

🐾 *The Cat Who Came for Christmas*, Cleveland Amory (Penguin, 1988). The true story of how a New York City gentleman's life was changed by a cat named Polar Bear.

🐾 *The Incredible Journey*, Sheila Burnford (Little, Brown and Co., 1961). The true story of two dogs and a cat who travel together across 200 miles of Canadian countryside to get home.

Want More?

🐾 If you've read through all of these books and still want more, there are also lots of magazines and comics out there for caring kids like you. Check out PETA's kids' magazine, *Grrr!* and all the free comics available at www.petakids.com, as well as all the great books at www.petabookstore.com. Share the World (www.sharetheworld.com) and www.justchoices.com also have lots of links to other animal rights and environmental publications.

🐾 If movies are what get you grooving, there are loads of animal-friendly titles you can check out on the video shelves too: *Charlotte's Web, Legally Blonde, Legally Blonde 2, Babe, Babe 2, Finding Nemo, Shark Tale, Wallace and Gromit, Let's Ask the Animals, Chicken Run, Free Willy, 101 Dalmatians, Stuart Little, Stuart Little 2, Dr. Doolittle,* and *Dr. Doolittle 2* are just some of the entertaining animal adventures to look out for.

🐾 Lots of cartoons you can watch on TV or on DVD also have characters who love and look out for animals. Cartoon Network's *Teen Titans* stars Greg Cipes as the voice of Beast Boy. Greg's a vegan and a big PETA supporter. The characters on *Hi Hi Puffy Ami Yumi* declared in one episode that they would never participate in cruel activities like bullfighting, because they wouldn't want to hurt the bull. Nickelodeon's *Danny Phantom* has a vegetarian character and in one episode they even battle the ghost of a lunch lady who tries to force the cafeteria to sell meat after the kids have had meat banned! And not only is *The Powerpuff Girls'* own cosmetics brand cruelty-free, but Bubbles is a true animal friend who loves veggie burgers.

CHAPTER 39

Reflecting on Dissecting

"The kids should have a choice whether they want to dissect an animal or not. The point is to learn. You'll still learn the same way if there's a good alternative. So why should you have to abuse an animal?"

—Gerard Way, My Chemical Romance

Your teacher wants you to dissect. You decide to study:
   a. A cat.
   b. A rat.
   c. A Ribbit.

What could be more painless than "dissecting" a Ribbit—a cloth model frog? When you open the Ribbit frog's Velcro-fastened tummy, you see all the differently colored organs inside. Teachers all over the country have used Ribbit and other models, books, and computer programs to replace dissections.

Did You Know?

🐾 Almost 6 million animals are used in classroom dissections every year. We are taught we should love animals, but many schools still require students to dissect. It doesn't make sense to kill frogs, worms, cats, mice, and pigs to study their bodies, especially when there are so many other ways to learn. Other science projects where the animals arrive alive still might mean they are killed in the end. Hatching experiments often result in abandoned chicks and ducklings, who are most often disposed of unkindly or sent to be processed for food.

🐾 Lots of students just won't dissect. Kids all over the country are working together and with teachers, parents, and other supportive adults to get dissection out of their classrooms. There are lots of organizations willing to help (see "Check It Out" in this chapter for some of their names and addresses).

🐾 Students at Santa Fe High School wanted to put an end to dissection in their entire district, so with the support of their teachers, they formed the Environmental and Animal Rights Society. They went before the superintendent's cabinet to inform her of all the computer-based virtual dissections, models, videos, and other learning tools that can be used as alternatives to animal dissections. The superintendent was impressed and commended the students for their research into dissection alternatives, and they even got the New England Anti-Vivisection Society to donate $3,500 worth of models and videos to their high school so there'd be no excuses.

What You Can Do

🐾 Talk to your teacher. Explain that you care about animals and don't want to harm them. It's important for your teacher to understand that you're not trying to get out of the lesson simply because you think it's gross (although it is!) or that you don't want to do the work. There is a good chance he or she has a more interesting project you can work on, but you might suggest one yourself. Chances are, others in your class don't feel comfortable cutting up animals and wish they had an alternative. Encourage them to speak up about their feelings. You might want to start a petition for the right to a "violence-free" education.

🐾 Tell your parents how you feel—they can support you. Explain your reasons for objecting and they're sure to understand! Check out the alternatives, including computer models, models made of cloth, templates, diagrams, books, filmstrips, and videotapes. Alternatives can be reused by students for years to come, they don't smell, and they don't get thrown out with the trash!

🐾 If your teacher insists that you dissect, ask him or her to meet with you and your parents to discuss your concerns. If your instructor still won't budge, ask to meet with your principal.

SHE DID IT!

Laurie Wolff is the student responsible for getting the student choice policy passed in Clark County, Nevada. In April of 2002 when she was 13 years old, she campaigned against dissection for 2 years. When she was in Sixth grade, this straight-A student refused to dissect an earthworm and received a C for the assignment. According to her grandmother, Louise Anderson, who helped her with her campaign, she was inspired by an article she saw in *Grrr!* magazine. Because of her efforts, thousands of students now have a choice to learn without cruelty. The Clark County School District is the seventh largest district in the United States, with nearly 300 schools.

🐾 If you find out that your class will be taking part in a hatching experiment, suggest to your teacher that you use some of the many cruelty-free alternatives that are available instead. You'll find some at the United Poultry Concerns Web site (www.upc-online.org/hatching/activities.html), including information about a book titled *Egg: A Photographic Story of Hatching,* by Robert Burton, which shows chickens, ducklings, ostriches, and other birds, along with reptiles, fish, and insects, developing inside and hatching from an egg. You can also contact United Poultry Concerns at P.O. Box 150, Machipongo, VA 23405-0150, or by e-mail: info@upc-online.org.

Check It Out

🐾 Go to www.petakids.com and readup on dissection alternatives and facts to help you win arguments with people who are against trying them. Get your free comic book, *A Rat's Life,* and order some stickers to decorate your folders with messages like RATS HAVE RIGHTS and CUT CLASS—NOT FROGS. At www.petaliterature.org you can also order a CUT OUT DISSECTION locker poster and *Cut Out Dissection* leaflets to share with your classmates.

🐾 There are now dozens of alternatives to cruel dissections such as Froguts Virtual Dissection Software, which allows you to dissect and reconstruct an anatomically correct frog—as many times as you like! You can find out more about Froguts at www.froguts.com. Another fun alternative to learn with is the Netfrog Interactive Dissection Site at http://curry.edschool .virginia.edu/go/frog/Frog2/home.html, where you can take part in an on-line photographic dissection.

🐾 Contact animal protection groups that are ready to give you free advice and information. Make a free phone call to the Dissection Hotline at 1-800-922-FROG. You'll talk to people who have refused to dissect and have all kinds of helpful advice. There is also a Dissection E-Hotline, a free Internet discussion group for individuals who face ethical or moral objections to

HE DID IT!

Tim Eisemann, 13, was horrified when he learned that his school was sending ducklings from a hatching project to a slaughterhouse. Although his teacher didn't want to help him, Tim found a home for the ducklings at a wildlife rehabilitation center. "School hatching projects are wrong," Tim says. "They are inhumane, they don't teach students very much, and there are many alternatives."

animal dissection or vivisection, which can be found at http://
groups.yahoo.com/group/NAVSCompassionateStudents.

🐾 For more information and links to books and videos that
promote dissection alternatives, contact the Humane Society
of the United States at 2100 L St. NW, Washington, DC 20037
or call 202-452-1100. You can check out their humane education pages at www.hsus.org/animals_in_research/animals_
in_education/.

🐾 Contact the American Anti-Vivisection Society through their
Web site at www.aavs.org to gather more information on
vivisection alternatives and follow the links to www
.humanestudent.org, and www.animalearn.org, which is a
resource for students and teachers interested in stopping the
use of animals in classrooms. Animalearn also operates a
Science Bank, a free loan program offering innovative software and educational products to educators and students interested in exploring dissection alternatives.

🐾 Ask the New England Anti-Vivisection Society (NEAVS) for
the addresses of companies that have programs, models, and
films. You can contact them at www.neavs.org, e-mail them
at info@neavs.org, or write to New England Anti-Vivisection
Society, 333 Washington St., Suite 850, Boston, MA 02108.

Remember, *no one* should force you to hurt or kill an animal.
Others may not seem to understand, but with the facts and the alternatives, they will learn from your determination and compassion.

CHAPTER 40

Step Up on Your Soapbox

Your teacher wants you to give a speech in front of the class. You tell your classmates:

a. How to make a necklace out of bubblegum wrappers.
b. That "orangutan" means "person of the forest"—and how neat and gentle great apes are!

If your answer is b, you're our kind of animal!

Did You Know?

🐾 If the idea of giving a speech makes you feel like the embarrassed zebra who was black and white and red all over, you're not alone. Surveys have shown that speaking in public is one of the top fears of people in America!

🐾 Even Abraham Lincoln, a terrific speaker, probably had knocking knees and sweaty palms the first few times he stood up in front of people. Practice makes perfect: give lots of speeches and you'll get used to standing up there in front of the class—or a whole assembly! You'll also give lots of people something to think about.

🐾 When Jazmyn Cherie Wilburn had to give a persuasive speech to her college communications and public speaking class, she used PETA facts, leaflets, stickers, and videos to prove her point: A vegetarian diet is best! Not only did she receive an A on her speech, the then-13-year-old even convinced 4 of her 20-to-46-year-old classmates to go vegetarian on the spot.

🐾 PETA's education co-coordinator, Sangeeta Kumar, regularly gives speeches and video presentations to middle school students all over the country to teach them how important it is to respect animals. Here's what some of them had to say afterwards:

> "A lot of adults don't understand a subject as strong as this. If you teach the kids, the adults of the future will understand."
>
> "I'm considering making a change, maybe to stop buying products that were tested on animals."
>
> "I have been thinking about being a vegetarian for a while now, and this video, and the speaker, helped push this process further along for me."

🐾 Adam Locke, a high school student in California, arranged with a local TV station to tape a "Speak Out" message about a student's right to refuse to dissect animals. It didn't cost Adam a dime and was played on five different TV channels and a radio station!

What You Can Do

If you are going to give a speech, here are some tips:

- Choose one animal rights issue such as cosmetics testing, carriage horses, or the factory farming of chickens. It's hard to cover all aspects of even one animal abuse issue and the many reasons why animals need to be protected in five minutes!
- Be sure your speech has a beginning, a middle, and an end.
- Keep your sentences short and simple. You don't want to bore your audience—if they doze off, it will be hard to convince them of anything.
- Include specific examples. Mention companies that still use animal tests or show photographs of animals who got tangled in plastic trash. Members of your audience may otherwise have a hard time believing the problem.
- Tell listeners what they can do to help. If you talk about how animals are treated on farms, hand out tasty vegetarian recipes. If you discuss cosmetic testing, pass out lists of cruelty-free companies so your audience can get involved. The animals won't gain any friends if people don't know how to help.
- Practice a little to a live audience. Ask your family, friend, or even your dog or cat to listen to your speech, but don't rehearse too much or you'll sound like a computer.
- Talk to your teachers about getting a representative from a humane society or animal protection organization to speak to your class or attend speeches given by other people. You may pick up tips you can use, and you'll have a chance to bring up your favorite subject at question time.
- Call or write the managers of your local radio and television stations to see if the station will let you tape a "Speak Out" on an animal issue.

Check It Out

- 🐾 PETA's Web site at www.peta.org has links to lots of informative fact sheets that can be used for researching your assignments and their magazines, *Animal Times* and *Grrr!*, are always full of useful topics to research. For up-to-date information on PETA's animal activists—and how you can become involved in campaigns yourself—check out the www.petakids.com site.

- 🐾 Call your local humane society to find out if they have a humane educator. Ask your teacher to get a speaker (or a film) for your school assembly.

- 🐾 For more information you can contact the National Humane Education Society (www.nhes.org) by e-mail at nhesinformation@nhes.org, or by writing to P.O. Box 340, Charles Town, WV 25414-0340. They offer a directory of education resources—and run an essay contest for kids, too!

CHAPTER
41

Lost and Found

One night a little cat named Moomin climbed out an open window and went to investigate a fascinating smell coming from the other side of the street. It was so late that the street was very quiet, and Moomin didn't realize she'd done something dangerous. When it began to rain, she scrunched up under a bush to keep dry. The rain stopped when morning came but by then the street was full of cars carrying people to work and school. Moomin heard her companions calling for her, but she was too scared of the traffic to cross back. Hungry and wet, she crept through the neighborhood, looking for another way back, but before she knew it, she was lost.

That night Moomin fell asleep under a porch, exhausted. The barks of strange dogs kept waking her, and she jumped a mile when she saw a raccoon family come out of the storm sewer to look for food. For the first time in her life she was cold and her stomach ached. All she could do was hope.

Moomin's story is true. Her guardians did find her, but only because they searched for twelve days and did everything you will read in this chapter. It takes love and persistence, but having your friend home safe and sound will be worth the work.

Did You Know?

🐾 Dogs and cats can easily get lost, especially if a storm frightens them or rain causes them to lose the scent of the way back home.

🐾 About 2 million dogs are stolen each year. Some thieves sell them to research laboratories or fight trainers or as "guard dogs." According to a detective who tracks lost dogs, some animals have even been kidnapped and held for ransom.

🐾 Fewer animals are stolen in winter than in summer when days are longer and more animals are left outside longer.

🐾 Domestic dogs and cats are sometimes stolen and killed for their fur, which is then labeled as "wolf" or "rabbit" and used to trim hats, coats, scarves, and gloves.

What You Can Do

🐾 The best thing to do is to help your companion not to get lost in the first place. Never leave animals alone in cars, tied in front of stores, or even in your own backyard, unless people you trust are watching out for them. Thieves look in these places and only need a few seconds to take an animal.

🐾 Fix places in your fence where animals can squeeze through. Put up a PLEASE CLOSE THE GATE sign.

🐾 Cats can roam long distances, so keep them safe and sound inside your home or screened porch. If you feel they must go out, buy cat-safe harnesses and long leashes, and let them go out and enjoy the yard whenever you do.

🐾 Make sure dogs and cats always wear easy-to-see identification. Attach an ID tag securely to the animal's collar, and have your companion *microchipped* (see below).

🐾 An ID tag for cats or young puppies can be hooked to a collar made out of sewing elastic, which won't strangle the animal if caught on a hook or tree limb. Sticky glow-in-the-dark tape can be put on the collar to make your friend more visible at night.

✸ A *microchip* is a very small electronic device that can be programmed with information in the same way that files are stored on a computer disk. It is inserted just under your cat or dog's skin and is so tiny it does not hurt. The microchip is programmed with information, such as your name and contact details, which can be scanned at a vet clinic or shelter if an animal is taken in. It is always a good idea to microchip your companion animals as well as attaching an ID tag to their collars. You can have your animal friend microchipped at your local veterinary clinic or animal shelter.

✸ Take several photos of your animal friend now. They should show any unusual markings, a close-up of his or her face, as well as the whole animal.

✸ If allowed in your community, post sturdy signs that tell thieves they will be seen, such as THIEF! OUR PETS ARE BEING WATCHED!

✸ Visit www.peta.org to download free fact sheets on companion animal care and visit www.helpinganimals.com for more ways to be aware of the needs of animals in your neighborhood and of our native wildlife.

✸ If an animal turns up missing, look everywhere, and look again every day. Here's how:

  • Visit area animal shelters daily. Leave a description and photo at each one.

  • Check the lost-and-found section of your newspapers.

  • Put up LOST posters on trees, telephone poles, and bulletin boards. Give the animal's name and description and your phone number. If possible, put up a current photo of him or her.

  • Call local veterinarians.

  • Ask mail carriers, neighbors, and construction workers in your area for their help. These people are out and about in places and at times when you aren't and may have seen— and can keep a lookout for—your companion.

- Call out to the animal at night when it's quiet, and you might hear even a faint reply.
- Look under houses, call and listen at openings to drainage ditches, and look up in trees. Cats can squeeze into very small places and get stuck.
- Spray-paint big, simple messages on scrap lumber and place these signs at intersections where drivers can't miss them. Keep it simple, like BLACK DOG LOST, CALL 555-4566.
- Offer a reward on your signs and in your ads. If you have an answering machine, tape a message with a description of your lost friend. Be sure your recording says when someone will answer in person. Thieves don't leave phone numbers!
- If school is in session, ask at the office of all the local schools to post a notice on the bulletin board and make an announcement over the loudspeaker.
- Go door to door in your neighborhood with flyers.
- Contact all local laboratories and animal dealers (your local humane society or animal rights group should have a list of them). The federal Animal Welfare Act allows you to go inside and look for a lost animal. If you have trouble, you should call the police and/or the humane society for help.
- Check with sanitation crews who remove dead animals from roads.
- If you've moved recently, do everything you're doing in your new area in your old neighborhood, too. Sometimes, confused by a move, companion animals have traveled far to return to their old homes.
- Organize a Theft Watch team with other concerned kids.
- Keep a file of the animals in your neighborhood (where they live, their names, descriptions, and so on). Tell neighbors what you're doing and warn them of the dangers of leaving animals alone outside. Try to get a photo of each animal.
- Distribute ID tag order forms (available at most veterinary clinics and animal shelters).

CHAPTER

42

It's Your Turn to Set the Table

Question: What has four legs, goes to the mall, and spreads the word about animal rights?
Answer: Your animal rights information table.

Did You Know?

🐾 You can have a great time at the mall without spending a penny. Malls aren't just for shopping or hanging out anymore—they're for animal rights activities too.

🐾 You can introduce tons of people to animal rights issues at fairs and festivals in your town.

🐾 You can fill petitions with hundreds of signatures in just a few hours at concerts, college student unions, malls, fairs, or any other place where lots of people will see you.

🐾 You can help inform others without speaking a word. How? By setting up a table display at your library!

What You Can Do

Plan early:

🐾 If you want to set up an animal tights information table at a fair or festival, make sure to call the mayor's office or the police station to see if you need permission and if there are any rules you need to follow. You might have to fill out a form, and it could take a few weeks to get approval.

🐾 To table at a mall, you simply need permission from the mall manager (to avoid problems later, get it in writing).

🐾 Check with the librarian at your school's library or at your town's public library—you may be able to display information for several weeks.

You'll need to get supplies and information:

🐾 If you don't have a card table, borrow one from a neighbor or look for one at flea markets or thrift stores in your area. Cover it with a clean sheet.

🐾 You can make posters with photographs and information clipped out of animal rights newsletters and glued onto poster board. Poster board can be found in almost any art supply shop.

🐾 It's easy to make a donation can to keep on your table. Just use a clean, empty can. Cut a money slot into a plastic lid. You can make a label by wrapping paper around the can and decorating it with animal rights messages and your group's name. If you're collecting money for a specific organization, say so.

🐾 You can make petitions to have people sign. At the top, write a simple description of what the petition is about—a local event, such as pig wrestling, or a business, such as horse-drawn carriages. Then draw lines across the rest of the page for people to sign their names, addresses, and signatures. Make sure you put a number (starting at 1 on each page) beside the signature line, otherwise your signatures will not be counted. Your petition should look something like this:

WE, the undersigned, ask the county government to ban pig wrestling from the county fair and other events held in our county:

   Name   Address   Signature

1. ————————————————————————————————

2. ————————————————————————————————

3. ————————————————————————————————

❀ Once the petition is full of signatures, present it to the county council. Call the city hall to find out who the council chairperson is and how you can make an appointment to meet with her or him. You can tell the local newspaper what you're doing and they might want to interview you about the problem.

Remember:

❀ To flash a smile so people who pass your table will feel more comfortable about coming up to you for information.

❀ Don't slouch—stand up straight! No one will be interested in your information if you're slumped over on a chair. They'll think it put even *you* to sleep!

❀ If you have friends helping you, zip your lips! Of course you can talk to each other, but don't ignore people who visit your table. They might be very interested and have important questions they need you to answer.

🐾 Don't argue with rude people. Offer to give them information to take with them. If you spend too much time talking to someone who doesn't care, you might miss a chance to talk to someone who does!

You'll be surprised how eager people are to learn how they can help animals. But don't be discouraged if a few people are unfriendly. Some people don't want to care about animals because they may have to make changes in their lives. Concern for animals is growing, and one day even those people will probably understand and agree with you.

Check It Out

🐾 Write to PETA at 501 Front St., Norfolk, VA 23510 or call 757-622-PETA to request brochures on any animal rights topic covered by their many campaigns. You can also log on to www.petaliterature.com to view all the brochures and fact sheets available to order and download. The Web site www.petakids.com often has on-line and downloadable petitions you can print off and distribute, so be sure to search that site too!

🐾 If you are over 13 or have older brothers and sisters, find out about Peta2. Peta2 is PETA's animal rights group for teens, which is based around the Peta2 Street Team—young people who promote animal rights in their local communities through leafleting and protesting at public youth events such as music concerts and tours. Check out the cool site and join the Street Team to receive info and updates on all their activities at www.peta2.com.

CHAPTER 43

School's Out!

First Kid: "Heard you're taking a mountain-climbing class this summer!"
Second Kid: "Yes. My mother says I've got to bring my grades up above C level!"

Some kids learn as much during their summer vacations as they do when they're in school. Somehow, learning is a lot more fun—and easy—when you're studying something you *really* like. You might use some of your vacation time to learn about animals and their habitats, for example. When school's back in session, don't be shy about sharing your new knowledge and skills with your classmates!

Did You Know?

There are lots of things you can do that do animals a good turn, even when you're vacationing:

- 🐾 Cutting back on the amount of meat you eat is a great way to help animals. Vacations are good times to explore new foods and try new recipes.
- 🐾 If you're already a vegetarian or vegan, or are becoming one, you might want to look to meet other kids who don't eat animals and who won't make fun of you for eating barbecued tofu!
- 🐾 Starting a club is one way to meet kids with your interests—or you can go to an overnight summer camp that serves only vegetarian food.
- 🐾 Closer to home, try joining in on animal protection programs that let you work alongside shelter staff, learning how to care for companion animals and doing other animal-related activities.

What You Can Do

Consider attending an overnight camp that supports vegetarianism and/or encourages compassion for animals:

- 🐾 Legacy International is an overnight camp that offers programs focusing on peace, tolerance, and compassion—and offers vegetarian food. It is for kids ages 8 to 10 and each session lasts 1 or 2 weeks and includes games, stories, group meetings, field trips, and special guests. Check out their summer program site at www.globalyouthvillage.org, write to Legacy International, 1020 Legacy Dr., Bedford, VA 24523, phone 540-297-5982, or e-mail mail@legacyintl.org.
- 🐾 In Canada, Au Grand Bois (French for "in the great woods") offers campers lots of games and outdoor activities and also

serves vegetarian food. Visit http://agb.ottawa.com/, or e-mail agb@magma.ca for more information.

🐾 If you live in Massachusetts, you can join the Massachusetts Society for the Prevention of Cruelty to Animals statewide summer programs. The MSPCA Nevins Farm Children's Summer Camp program runs 4 2-week sessions for children entering grades 2 through 8. The eighth-grade session is a more in-depth program covering animal protection and environmental issues. For more information, call 978-687-7453 or visit www.mspca.org.

🐾 The St. Louis Humane Society's Critters Camp, for kids aged 7 to 12, teaches humane treatment of animals. Contact the Humane Society of Missouri at www.hsmo.org, or you can call them at 314-647-8800 or write to 1201 Macklind Ave., St. Louis, MO 63110.

🐾 The Peninsula Humane Society in San Mateo, California, runs Humane Helpers, an after-school program for 10-to-12-year-olds one Thursday a month, from September to May. You can learn about different animal-related topics and about some essential functions of the humane society. The group also completes simple service projects to help the animals. They also run Animal Camp, an intensive, week-long camp for 9-to-12-year-olds that shows responsible companion animal care and lets kids see how important all species are. Contact www.peninsulahumanesociety.org or call 650-340-7022.

🐾 The San Francisco Society for the Prevention of Cruelty to Animals (SFSPCA) offers a Middle School Career Exploration Week and summer camps from grades 5 through 9 from June to August. Dog and Cat Camp includes daily hands-on play and work with cats and dogs. Each day campers play with kittens and cats, help walk and train dogs, as well as carry out other activities, demonstrations, games, and projects. Contact the SFSPCA Humane Education Department at 415-554-3065, e-mail humaneeducation@sfspca.org, or visit www.sfspca.org for more information.

🐾 The Marin Humane Society runs a Junior Animal Camp for first- and second-graders with animal-centered arts and crafts, fun, and games. They also run the Animal Care Camp for third and fourth grades, and Senior Animal Care Camp for fifth and sixth grades. All camps run several sessions from July through August. Call 415-883-4621, ext. 308, to request an application or write to Animal Care Camp, the Marin Humane Society, 171 Bel Marin Keys Blvd., Novato, CA 94949. You can also find out more at www.marin-humane.org.

Check It Out

🐾 Write or call your local humane society, animal shelter, or animal rights group to find out about animal protection programs and camps for kids in your area.

🐾 Start a club! Summer vacation is the perfect time to get a bunch of kids together and form a group for animals. See Chapter 48, "Join the Club," for great ideas on how you can do just this!

🐾 Call, write, or drop in to your local shelter to find out what you can do to lend a hand. The staff might be eager to have you walk the dogs, play with the cats, clean cages, fill water bowls, and more. You can usually help out by collecting and donating the materials shelters never seem to have enough of, such as old blankets, towels, sheets, newspaper, and leashes.

Remember that all the information on programs in this chapter is likely to change at least a little bit over time. Be sure to contact the programs for more details and up-to-date information on what they offer when you are ready to attend.

CHAPTER 44

Develop a Good Roadside Manner

Little kindnesses matter all by themselves. When you fall and hurt yourself, it would be awful if people decided they were too busy to stop and help. It's important to take time for any animal who is in trouble too, no matter where you are going or how rushed you are.

How Do You Rate?

Are you a savvy roadside savior? Take a quick quiz and find out:

1. You are playing in your front yard when you see a dog running down the middle of the street without a lead on or an owner. You:
   a. Get your mom to help you catch the dog and keep him in your front yard while you check for a phone number on

his collar tag and call the owner so they can come and collect him.

b. Keep watching to see if he's going to get hit when the next car comes.

c. Stay playing in the garden because the dog looked like he knew where he was going.

2. You are in the car with your parents and you see a squirrel lying still at the side of the road. You:

a. Ask them to turn around and go back so you can get out and check if the squirrel is dead or just hurt and needs help.

b. Think it serves the squirrel right—roads are for cars!

c. Feel sad but don't say anything.

3. A cat wanders into your backyard without a collar or tag on. You:

a. Take her to the local vet or animal shelter to be scanned for microchip identification and put up "found" notices in the neighborhood.

b. Pick her up and throw her back over the fence.

c. Watch her wander around until she moves on into the neighbor's garden.

4. You find an opossum dead under a tree in your school yard. You:

a. Get a teacher to help you call out a wildlife rehabilitator in case the opossum is female and has a pouch full of living babies.

b. Poke her with a stick because it's funny.

c. Get the cleaner to pick her up and dispose of her.

Mostly a's Super-Saver on site! You are always on the lookout for an animal in trouble and take the right action when you find one needing help. You also know who to go for if you can't do it all alone and involve your friends and family in the rescue. Congratulations: you're the animals' best friend in your neighborhood.

Mostly b's A little lazy on the rescue run? 'Fraid so. Animals are often confused and need help if they are hurt or lost—you need to have a heart for animals and stop thinking humans rule! Try to put yourself in the position of an animal, like a lost cat, and think how you would feel and how you'd hope to be treated.

Mostly c's Halfway's not the most helpful way! You're not totally useless to an animal in need, but you don't always go the extra mile to do what's best for the animal. Don't be afraid to ask for help from parents or teachers if you think an animal might need assistance, and always remember that if animals are hurt or lost, they *do* need your help.

Did You Know?

Dogs and cats are sometimes abandoned along the road or at highway rest areas by people who imagine the animals will somehow learn to fend for themselves:

- Eva-Jean Fridh of Georgetown, Texas, saw a dog alone at a rest area early one summer. She didn't stop because she thought that the dog was just waiting for someone to come out of the rest room. Many weeks later, Eva-Jean and her family by chance ended up at the same rest area—to find the same dog there! The dog was weak with hunger and thirst, was bitten all over by fire ants, and couldn't even stand up. Eva-Jean knew what she had to do. She brought the dog home, nursed her back to health, and named her Sandy. Sandy is full of energy today. Her coat is soft and shiny, and her eyes sparkle with joy. Eva-Jean and her family saved Sandy's life, and now Sandy makes their lives even happier!

- Sometimes animals who have been hit on the highway are not dead, but unconscious or unable to get up and move away. It's always best to check if you have any doubt. Ask your parents to stop and when it's safe walk back with you to check on and care for an injured animal.

🐾 "If you're ever out and see an injured animal, call your local wildlife rehabilitator or animal control number right away. It's a good idea to always have this number handy," writes one young PETA member. "When I was riding my bicycle I came across an injured pigeon. He was in terrible shape. The front of his chest was bloody and his beak was broken. It looked like he had either been hit by a car or attacked by a cat. I called PETA's Community Animal Project emergency number and they came out right away to help him out. Turns out he was attacked by a cat, so also remember to keep your companion animals indoors where they are safe from the streets. I found this pigeon on the side of a very busy road and the cat that attacked him was lucky to not have ended up there too."

What You Can Do

🐾 If you see a dog or cat running along the side of the road or hanging around a fast-food place or rest area, call Information for the local humane society's phone number and report the situation. If the road is busy or the weather is bad, try to wait until they arrive if you are able, or at least check back later to see if the animal is still there. If the animal is in danger of being hit by a car or picked up by a person with bad intentions, try to get him or her to come to you by using kind words and perhaps some food, and then take the animal home or to the local animal shelter.

🐾 Someone could be looking for their pal, so put up simple FOUND signs on telephone polls, on bulletin boards, and in other public places. Give your phone number, but don't describe the animal in detail. You can only be certain the people who call you are the animal's true guardians if they can describe their companion completely. See Chapter 41, "Lost and Found," for more information on what to do with lost animals.

🐾 Stock your family's car with an animal rescue kit: a medium-size box with air holes punched in it, a blanket, some thick gloves, the phone numbers and addresses of veterinarians and wildlife rehabilitators, and a leash.

🐾 Call around to find out which veterinarians are open on evenings and weekends and which may treat lost, injured animals for free if you explain the situation, and which will require that you pay. You may want to have a fund-raiser or gather donations so that you will have funds on hand to take care of a stray animal emergency.

🐾 Birds are often stunned by cars. Any birds found on or at the side of the road should be picked up very gently, put into a box with air holes punched in it or a paper sack with the top folded over, then taken to a wildlife rehabilitator. Birds are terrified of people, so don't let anyone hold them, pet them, or make a lot of noise, and don't stare at them.

🐾 When you see animals lying at the side of the road, always take the time to stop and check whether they're still alive. You should do this without touching the animals, because that might startle or hurt them more. If you aren't sure if they're still breathing, here's how to check:

- First, of course, make absolutely sure you are in no danger from traffic. If it is safe for the animal to be left where he is, it is best not to move him, as you may accidentally hurt him. If he is in danger of traffic, for example, get a grown-up to help you remove the animal very gently, using gloves or a towel, to the safety of the curb, away from the pavement.

- You may be able to see light breathing by looking at an animal's chest. If not, take a twig or a piece of rolled-up newspaper and, very gently, touch the inner corner of the animal's eye. If there is any movement, she or he is alive. If not, you have helped anyway, because crows, opossums, and other animals who clean the Earth by surviving on carcasses won't be killed while eating.

🐾 If you can tell that the animal on the road is alive but badly hurt, flag down a police officer or call the humane society.

Ask people to help get the animal to the side of the road gently and carefully. Animals who are hurt and scared can bite in self-defense. Try to have someone stay with the animal at all times.

🐾 If you find a female opossum you know is dead, call a wildlife rehabilitator and ask them to check to see if she has a pouch full of babies. Since opossums carry their babies in stomach pouches, the babies may not have been hurt in the accident. If you find babies, keep them all together in a small box with air holes punched in it and on a soft towel, and call the nearest wildlife rehabilitator as soon as possible. These babies need very special care that only a wildlife rehabilitator can give them (contact the local humane society or animal control office for the name of a wildlife rehabilitator). Of course, the best thing to do is prevent animals from being hit by cars in the first place! Here are some ideas:

- Get your class to write letters to the mayor asking that barriers such as concrete slabs be put up along local roads and highways where you see a lot of animals hurt (your local library or city council Web site has the mayor's name and address).

- Encourage your city officials to prevent cars from hitting animals by keeping grass, shrubs, and trees cut back from the roadside at least several feet. When plants are put right next to the road, they attract animals who eat them or who are looking for places to live.

- And, of course, do not let "companimals" outside without a leash and without supervision unless they're in a fenced-in yard (dogs) or a screened-in porch (cats).

Check It Out

🐾 Write to Friends of Animals for a bumper sticker that reads CAUTION: I BRAKE FOR ANIMALS to put on your family's car. See www.friendsofanimals.org, write to 777 Post Rd., Suite 205, Darien, CT 06820, or call 203-656-1522.

🐾 For fact sheets and more information on why dogs and cats should be kept indoors unless supervised, visit www.peta.org, write to PETA 501 Front St., Norfolk, VA 23510, or call 757-622-PETA. PETA also has a Web site at www.helpingwildlife.com, where you can find out many more ways to be active for wildlife.

🐾 For more information about wildlife rehabilitation and to find a rehab center or certified "rehabber" near you, contact the following organizations. Write them before an emergency comes up, so you'll be prepared:

- International Wildlife Rehabilitation Council (IWRC): Visit www.iwrc-online.org, write to P.O. Box 8187, San Jose, CA 95155, call 408-271-2685, or e-mail office@iwrc-online.org.
- National Wildlife Rehabilitators Association (NWRA): Visit www.nwrawildlife.org, write to 2625 Clearwater Rd., Suite 110, St. Cloud, MN 56301, or call 320-230-9920.

Here's a short list of regional wildlife rehabilitation centers you can turn to for help:

HOWL: The PAWS Wildlife Center
www.paws.org
P.O. Box 1037, Lynnwood, WA 98046
E-mail: info@paws.org
Phone: 425-787-2500

The Northwoods Wildlife Center
www.northwoodswildlifecenter.com
8683 Blumenstein Rd.—Highway 70, West Minocqua, WI 54548
E-mail: edu@northwoodswildlifecenter.com
Phone: 715-356-7400

Peninsula Humane Society Wildlife Center
www.peninsulahumanesociety.org/services/wild.html
12 Airport Blvd., San Mateo, CA 94401
Phone: 650-340-7022

Wildlife Rescue, Inc.
www.wildliferescueinc.org
19406 Grave Run Rd., Hampstead, MD 21074
Phone: 443-507-0950

University of Minnesota Wildlife Rehabilitation Clinic
www.wrcmn.org
2530 Dale St. N., Roseville, MN 55113
Phone: 651-486-9453

Willowbrook Wildlife Haven
525 S Park Blvd., Glen Ellyn, IL 60137
Phone: 630-942-6200

Wildlife Center of Virginia
www.wildlifecenter.org
P.O. Box 1557, Waynesborough, VA 22980
E-mail: wildlife@wildlifecenter.org
Phone: 540-942-9453

Chesapeake Wildlife Sanctuary
www.homestead.com/chesapeakewildlife
17308 Queen Anne Budge Rd., Bowie, MD 20716
Phone: 301-390-7010

Suncoast Seabird Sanctuary
www.seabirdsanctuary.org
18328 Gulf Blvd., Indian Shores, FL 33785
E-mail: seabird@seabirdsanctuary.org
Phone: 727-391-6211

Wildlife Rescue Association
www.wildliferescue.ca
5216 Glencarin Dr., Burnaby, BC V5B Canada
E-mail: wildlife@vcn.bc.ca
Phone: 604-526-2747

CHAPTER 45

Add a Little Spice
to Their Lives

Who likes pasta, garbanzo beans, peas, corn, fruit,
and rice?

    a. Dogs
    b. Cats
    c. People
    d. All of the above

Letter d is correct! We all like variety in our diets! In
fact, dogs even like garlic—but that might make their
bark worse than their bite!

In the jungles of the Gombe, in Tanzania, Africa, members of chimpanzee families spend many hours each day gathering food. In one
month they can collect and eat as many as forty to sixty different
kinds of leaves, roots, fruits, and seeds from trees with names like

Ipomoea, Dalbergia, and Harungana. Some foods taste very sweet, while others are quite bitter. Some things these great apes chew on are natural medicines; chimpanzees, like many tribal humans, seem always to have known how to find and pick natural, herbal remedies to treat their illnesses and injuries!

Did You Know?

🐾 Some pet food companies like Iams and Sergeant's Pet Care actually test their products on animals. That doesn't mean feeding yummy food to a happy dog—it means frightened, lonely dogs and cats confined to tiny cold cages having horrible things done to them in laboratories. Tests include cutting huge chunks of muscle from dogs' legs, and de-barking them. Cats are infected with fatal diseases and left to die in pain. These tests are not necessary and they are not required by law. For more information and ways you can help stop this, visit www.petakids.com/iams.html.

🐾 Just like chimpanzees, dogs in the wild, whether dingos of Australia, pariah dogs of Asia, or wolves and foxes in the Americas, eat a very varied diet. Just like people too, all dogs may fancy a particular taste one day and something different the next. Canids (that's the dog family name) are taught by their mothers to select many varieties of wild berries and to hunt for small creatures. But like captive chimpanzees who can't get out of the zoo or the laboratory, dogs and cats and other animals who live with humans have no choice; they eat what they're given day after day. Many dogs and cats kept in human households eat just one kind of food, often some sort of boring canned glop or dry pellets, for their whole lives. That's pretty dull!

Of course, letting companion animals outdoors in our busy, built-up world wouldn't work. Not only are there precious few of the right kind of berry bushes for them to feed on and wild creatures to hunt, but no one taught them as youngsters that those kinds of things are edible. Our friends would probably starve.

Never fear: you can help! Pep up your cat's or dog's (or even hamster's) diet by baking or "foraging" for them:

What You Can Do

- 🐾 Please them with pasta! You'd think most dogs come from Italy because they really love spaghetti (with a little tomato sauce) and other noodle dishes. Fresh garlic is not only good for dogs (it's a blood cleanser and a flea and tick repellent), but sprinkled on food it can be a big hit with the canine crowd. Like pasta, rice is not only good for dogs, but most of them enjoy it as long as it is mixed with something tasty (like noodles, bread, or kibble).
- 🐾 Mix it up with gravies! Brown gravies and barbecue sauces are often a big hit with dogs and cats. Mashed cooked carrots, cooled down, and nutritional yeast get rave reviews from some other-than-humans.
- 🐾 Cut up in the kitchen! Fresh-cut carrots (raw, this time) and chunks of washed apple or pear are liked not only by dogs who like to crunch, but also by hamsters, mice, rats, rabbits, and gerbils. Unsalted nuts are also usually gladly gobbled. Try giving them in the shell. If cracking the shell seems too tough for your friend, shelled unsalted nuts do just fine. Best of all, some rodents like to eat wildflowers, like clover and dandelions.
- 🐾 Be a chef for a *chat* (that's French for "cat"). Cats' tastes vary a lot. Some cats like melon, others like rye bread pieces (a whole slice is usually too hard to manage), and lentil soup or soy milk are favorites of others.
- 🐾 Tempt them with tofu. Lots of dogs and cats enjoy bean curd mashed up with gravy or mixed with other foods. Here are two easy-to-fix recipes created specially for dogs and cats:

Dog Biscuits (PETA recipe collection)

4½ cups whole-wheat flour
½ cup nutritional yeast (check your local health food store)
½ tbsp. salt
½ tbsp. garlic powder

Mix dry ingredients. Add about 1½ cups water. Knead into a big ball of dough. Roll dough out with a rolling pin on a piece of wax paper until it is a big flat circle. Cut into shapes with your favorite cookie cutters. Put dog "cookies" on a cookie sheet and bake for 10–15 minutes with the oven set at 350° F. After all the biscuits are baked, leave them in the oven overnight so they get hard and crunchy.

Garbanzo Cat Chow (courtesy of Harbingers of a New Age)

1 can of cooked garbanzo beans (also called chickpeas—you can
   buy them at the grocery store)
1½ tbsps. nutritional yeast powder
1 tbsp. chopped or grated vegetables (lots of cats especially love
   corn!)
1 tbsp. oil
1 tsp. Vegecat supplement (ordering information at end of chapter)
1 tsp. soy sauce

Mix all the ingredients together and serve warm. They love it!

Follow these feeding tips:

🐾 Feed companion animals before you and your family eat. When they have to wait until afterward, dogs can get worried they've been forgotten and start asking for food during your meal.

🐾 When you've finished feeding, always say, "All gone," and give an upturned palms ("empty hands") signal, followed by a scratch behind the ears (theirs, not yours!).

Check It Out

🐾 You can order nutritional supplements for your dogs and cats from Harbingers of a New Age. Each order comes with a bunch of free recipes! If you want your cats and dogs to become vegetarians, you must include nutritional supplements in their food every day. All cats have nutritional needs that are met by the Vegecat supplement, which you can order from this company. You can write to them at 717 E. Missoula Ave., Troy, MT 59935, phone 406-295-4944, e-mail info@ vegepet.com, or visit their Web site at www.vegepet.com.

🐾 Write to PETA (501 Front St., Norfolk, VA 23510) or visit the site www.caringconsumer.com for a list of vegan pet food companies and those who do not test their products. A few of these are Natural Balance Pet Foods (1-800-829-4493; www.naturalbalanceinc.com), Natural Life Pet Products (1-800-367-2391; www.nlpp.com), and Evolution Diet (1-800-659-0104; www.petfoodshop.com).

CHAPTER 46

Make Sure Fair Is Fair

One little piggy was prodded and raced
Another little piggy was greased and chased
Yet a third little piggy was thrown to the ground
So this little piggy complained all around!

—Jonathan Canby, age eight

You and your friends probably love a trip to the annual fair. You like walking around all day, enjoying something tasty for lunch, and taking in the sights and the noise of the crowd. But are the animals in the exhibits at the fair having as much fun as you are?

How Do You Rate?

Take a quiz and find out if you're clued into fairground cruelty:

1. Just after you arrive at the fair, you come to an exhibit where people are making a mule jump off what looks like a diving board into a pool of water while everyone cheers. You:
   a. Think it's really funny to see the big splash as she falls and get your friends to wait up and watch for a while.
   b. Can't believe anyone would enjoy watching a mule being hurt like that and start thinking of ways you can make sure the exhibit isn't there again next year.

2. A few hours later, you come to a petting zoo where kids are trying to pick up the lambs and chasing the baby rabbits. You:
   a. Jump straight in and see how many rabbits you can catch too, while holding on to a lamb at the same time.
   b. Find the supervisors of the zoo and ask them to tell the kids to stop chasing the rabbits, then take down the company name so you can write them a complaint later.

3. As the sun sets, you start making your way toward the fair gates, where you notice a stall you hadn't seen before. When you go inside to take a look, it turns out to be a photo booth where people can have their picture taken with a monkey who wears a top hat. You:
   a. Ask your friends to lend you five dollars so you can get your photo taken too.
   b. Decide to take a photo of the monkey instead to send to your local humane society. He looks sad and has a sore on his leg from where he has been chained to a cage.

Mostly a's You can still be a party animal and help save them too! You love a good time with friends, so if you think about it for a split second, you'll realize that the animals should enjoy the same.

Mules don't belong in pools, baby lambs and rabbits want to be with their moms, and monkeys want to play in trees with their jungle buddies. None of them enjoy being exhibits. Keep reading and you'll find out why fairs aren't always fair.

Mostly b's Awesome Animal Angel alert! When it comes to helping the animals, you're aware and ready for action. Since you chose b's, you probably find it hard to believe that anyone *could* choose mostly a's. But the scary thing is, a lot of people don't know enough about animals; otherwise cruel fair exhibits would have gone out of business long ago. Keep reading to find out how your help can make it happen now!

Did You Know?

- 🐾 When "diving," mules are forced to climb a rickety ramp to a thirty-foot-high platform and then plunge into the water going thirty miles an hour, it hurts! If you've ever done a belly flop from the high diving board, you know how bad it must feel. Even water buffalo, who love a good soaking, wouldn't dive into the river. Large animals have to shift their weight carefully first so they don't hurt themselves.

- 🐾 Some traveling zoos use baby tigers and lions and charge people to have their pictures taken with the small cubs. They usually get rid of the animals when they grow too big—sometimes when they are just a few months old—by selling them to roadside zoos or to people who just want their skin!

- 🐾 Have you heard the dirty joke about the pig who wallowed in the mud? Pigs really are clean—they lie in the mud only when they need to cool off, but people at fairs sometimes cover them with grease and wrestle them. Most people would say that yanking on a dog's ears and tail and tackling them to the ground is cruel; why shouldn't this go for pigs, too?

- 🐾 Many "wrestling" bears and alligators have their teeth and claws removed so they can't hurt people who try to pin them down. Needless to say, those bears would rather be in the woods, and the alligators back in the swamps, than in cramped, hot cages.

🐾 Did you hear about the turtle who stopped racing the rabbit because he always lost by a hare? That might sound funny, but making animals race is really no laughing matter. Imagine being packed into a truck without air-conditioning and shipped all over the country—and only being taken out of your cage to be prodded around a racetrack in the scorching heat.

🐾 All kinds of animals are raced, including ducks, hogs, llamas, turtles, slugs, pigs, ostriches, turkeys, and crabs. Certainly animals who are raced would keep on running (or waddling or crawling or hopping) after they crossed the finish line, if they could!

🐾 Dancing chickens don't really know how to tango. They are often shocked into jumping around by a heated floor or even by jolts of electricity sent through wires in the floor.

🐾 Ponies used in carousel rides work long hours, walking around and around in the hot sun. There are no Gatorade breaks for carousel ponies—they're lucky if they even get a sip of water. That's because drinking and eating will mean a mess later, and the people are too lazy to pick up after the animals.

🐾 Baby animals used in traveling zoos are lonely, sad animals taken away from their mothers before they are ready to be on their own. Just like human babies, lion and tiger cubs need their mothers' help to learn about life until they are all grown up.

🐾 Exotic animals used in traveling zoos and wrestling acts sometimes wind up on hunting ranches (where people pay to "bag a trophy") when they get old. Pigs who are wrestled or raced can wind up as the main course as soon as they get big and their track days are over.

🐾 On a lighter note, Great American Duck Races (Phoenix, Arizona) rents out rubber ducks for charity fund-raiser races. Organizers rent the racing ducks and then round up sponsors to adopt the birds, offering prizes for the winners. In a lake or pond, people can keep track of and collect back all of the ducks, so it's loads of fun. However, we don't recommend "duck" races on a river because they could float to the ocean and be swallowed by sea animals.

What You Can Do

🐾 Steer clear of acts or events that use animals. If no one goes to petting zoos, animal wrestling events, or exhibits where chickens in little boxes dance and caged rabbits play the piano, people won't make money from these events. Then they'll find ways to make money *without* causing animals to suffer.

🐾 Ask people to think about what happens to "show animals." When they realize what the animals go through and that there are not many retirement homes for them, they may think twice about spending money at such events.

🐾 Complain to managers who book animal acts. Let them know that these events are no fun for animals: ponies don't enjoy going in circles for hours, and "diving" mules remember the fear and abuse they went through in order to learn to "dive." Animals just want to be left in peace.

🐾 Set up a face-painting booth at the county fair. As you paint whiskers and/or kind messages on fair-goers' faces, hand out literature that informs them about the mistreatment of animals.

Check It Out

🐾 If you are going to a fair where you know there will be petting zoos, pony rides, or tiger exhibits, contact PETA (501 Front St., Norfolk, VA 23510 or call 757-622-PETA) and request some leaflets to distribute. You can also download or order brochures at www.petaliterature.com.

🐾 If your town fair is planning animal races, contact the organizers and tell them that if animals wanted to be sports celebrities, they'd organize their own Olympics! Suggest human "crab," wheelbarrow, or gunnysack races instead.

🐾 People can have fun creating paper origami (pronounced "or-ee-gah-mee") frogs. Check out books on how to create origami animals at your local library and bookstores. You and your friends can make tons of cute and interesting paper animals in this ancient Japanese art form.

If you see animals performing, check for the following:

🐾 Do the animals have plenty of clean water? Are their cages and pens clean?
🐾 Can they stand up, sit down, and turn around comfortably? Do they have shade and shelter?
🐾 Are the animals chained by the legs?
🐾 Do they look healthy, or are they sick, tired, or thirsty? Are their coats shiny (a sign of good health)? Or do they have cuts, sores, or scars?

It can be helpful if you can take photographs of any animals who look sick or abused. Send the information to animal protection groups that can improve the conditions for the animals—and maybe even get them retired to a sanctuary or some other friendly place.

CHAPTER 47

Get Poetic

For poetry ideas sure to be treasured, not trashed, look to other-than-human beings for inspiration. We all have creative talents, whether or not we are aware of them and whether or not we develop them. Expressing your feelings creatively is fun and can influence other people's feelings about animals—and emotions are some of the most powerful forces on Earth!

Here's a limerick on being vegetarian from 10-year-old Samantha Marianyi, who sent her cute poem to the PETA Kids magazine, *Grrr!*:

> *I'm a girl named Sam.*
> *I never eat any ham.*
> *Not even one slice,*
> *It doesn't smell nice!*
> *A proud vegetarian I am!!*

If that's not enough to inspire you, read these pieces from a poem by 12-year-old Rishi R. Mehta, who is a junior member of PETA India:

> *I've often wondered why people*
> *Eat animals as dishes,*
> *Ranging from mammals*
> *To amphibians and fishes?*
>
> *If it is called cruel,*
> *For slaves to be beaten*
> *Then it is far more spiteful*
> *For a living being to be eaten!*

Did You Know?

- Some people are at their creative best in the morning.
- Others' creativity blossoms at night.
- It's handy to have paper and pen near your bed, in case you wake in the night with a good idea.

What You Can Do

- Write a story from a wolf's or other animal's point of view. If we could understand other animals' languages, what would we hear?

If you were a cat, or a dog, or some other-than-human animal, what would you say about:

- Why you love a certain human—or kids in general?
- What it's like to be hunted?
- What you would do if you could escape from your cage or get unchained?

🐾 Having fun playing together as a school of fish?

🐾 Why not to go near people?

🐾 Exploring the ocean as a young whale?

🐾 Leaving the nest and learning to fly?

Try your hand at subject, tanka, haiku, and cinquain poems:

🐾 Write a subject poem by placing the letters of the subject in a column. Then write a line about the subject for each letter. For example:

> **W**onderful
> **O**utcast
> **L**oyal to each other
> **F**eared

🐾 Tanka poems have five lines with five syllables in the first and third lines and seven syllables each in the second, fourth, and fifth lines. Here's one about a fish:

> *Yellow and white stripes*
> *undulating through rolling*
> *warm azure ocean,*
> *her eyes wide, sheer tail steering*
> *flawless innocence through life.*

🐾 Haiku poems were first written in Japan. They have three lines. The first and third lines have five syllables each, and the second line has seven syllables. The haiku poet Issa wrote this about 200 years ago:

> *Snail, my little man,*
> *Slowly!—oh very slowly—*
> *Climb up Fujisan*

🐾 Cinquain poems are five-line, unrhymed poems that are fun and easy to write. A cinquain can show an animal to be complete and important for his or her own sake, so it's a good way to write nicely about an animal many people dislike or fear. Use these guidelines from *Choices: The Farm and You* (The Athene Trust, 1989):

> Rat
> *1 noun (animal's name or title)*
> Curious friend
> *2 words describing the animal*
> Never hurt anyone
> *3 words expanding the idea*
> Wants to be happy
> *4 words describing how you feel about this animal*
> Misunderstood
> *1 word to sum up the poem*

Check It Out

🐾 Put your pen to paper and try a poem about an animal most people think is scary or ugly or silly or dirty. Let people know all animals are special!

🐾 Visit the www.petakids.com Web site for competitions and check out the current edition of the PETA Kids magazine, *Grrr!*, to find out about future art, design, poetry and essay-writing competitions to enter.

🐾 Go to www.sharetheworld.com and download some of their Just Choices activity sheets, which will give you exciting ways to become more aware of how to write the *right* way with respect for all living beings.

PANDA SCOUTS

Join the Club

Nathan Runkle of Ohio is a true friend to animals. When he was just seventeen, he founded the group Mercy for Animals. He travels all over the country to organize more than five different campaigns, as well as publishing a magazine called *Outrage*. He even asked for an animal costume for Christmas to use in his protests! You can find out more of his work by looking at his group's Web site at www.mercyforanimals.org.

Did You Know?

🐾 By starting an animal rights club, you can help animals, make new friends, and have a whale of a time!

🐾 Like you, most kids love animals and hate to see them suffer. Use this book to show as many of your friends as you can ways they can help animals. Then ask them to spread the word—you'll find you soon have a group of caring kids, faster than you think.

🐾 Two heads are better than one, and three are even better, but no number of people is too small to make a difference, as long as they really care about helping animals. One will do if you don't have two!

What You Can Do

🐾 Organize a few friends who are interested in helping animals. Decide whether your group wants to focus your efforts on a single issue, such as carriage horses or fur, or lots of different animal issues.

🐾 When your group has decided what to work on, pick a name that describes what your club is about, such as Animal Allies, Veggie Kids, or Friends of Carriage Horses. Then choose a motto like "Just say no to animal cruelty" or "Eat beans, not beings" or "We're the Ele-Friends."

🐾 Set up a table in a busy area to inform others, protest cruel activities, and gather names on petitions.

🐾 Set up a booth at your school's fair and paint whiskers, animal faces, or kind messages on people who stop by. Maybe you'll find new club members!

HE DID IT!

Eleven-year-old Kyle Jacobs thinks that felines are the cat's meow, so he founded a local group to help cats called the Hamilton Cat Association and writes its annual newsletter, *Paws for Thought*. Kyle has raised money for an animal hospital, rescues stray cats in his neighborhood, and was named 2005 Volunteer of the Year among local elementary school students. Me-wow!

🐾 The Mann Humane Society of Novato, California, suggests making a cheap banner with a sheet and markers or textile (fabric) paint (art stores usually have the right kind of markers and paint). Spread out the banner on top of newspapers (so you don't stain the floor) and make sure that there are no wrinkles. Print your animal rights message and, if you like, draw a picture of an animal. Use the banner to recruit new members at a school club fair, at demonstrations (you may need to cut slits in it if it's windy so it doesn't act like a sail), at fund-raisers for your group, or anywhere you want to stand up and be noticed.

🐾 Hold letter-writing parties (see Chapter 25, "Write On!"). Serve vegetarian food like apples and peanut butter, hummus and pita bread, or whatever your favorites are.

🐾 Do some fund-raising for your club, scrub a Bug (or a Cougar, Fox, or Rabbit!) at a weekend car wash or have a vegan bake sale, clean up your room and hold a garage sale, or announce a "favorite animal friend" photo contest at school. Contest entry fees of even $1 can all help the club.

🐾 Promote your fund-raiser by making and giving out flyers (make them simple, clear, and colorful so people will take and read them); putting up posters at the supermarket, school, churches, synagogues, and other community spots (with permission); spreading the news "word of mouth"; and writing in your school and local newspapers about what you are up to.

🐾 Once you have the money, you can buy art supplies, memberships to other organizations, subscriptions to animal magazines, stamps, paper and envelopes for mailings, and whatever else your club might need. You might consider donating what's left over to an animal protection group or local shelter.

Check It Out

🐾 Call PETA at 757-622-PETA or log on to www.peta.org or www.petakids.org to find out how you can join in on activities in your area and get help and information to start your own animal-saving club!

🐾 Join the Kindness Club. Members get a big packet of information, a membership card and pin, and a subscription to the club newsletter. Visit www.smythe.nbcc.nb.ca/kindness, write to 65 Brunswick St., Fredericton, NB E3B 1G5, Canada, phone 506-459-3379, or e-mail kindness@nb.aibn.com.

CHAPTER 49

Hang in There

So How Do You Rate Now?

Take a quick quiz and find out if you're a pro animal assistant after reading this book:

1. One of the most animal-saving things you can do all by yourself is:
    a. Start breeding puppies.
    b. Change to a vegan diet.
    c. Refuse to ride in cars.

2. When you go shopping for cosmetics and household products, you should:
    a. Always make sure that they have not been tested on animals and do not include animal ingredients.

   b. Make sure that they have been thoroughly tested.

   c. Take a re-usable cotton bag to carry them all in.

3. You are given a parka for Christmas that has a coyote fur collar. You:

   a. Love it!

   b. Return it to the store explaining the cruelty of fur production and how disgusted you are that they sell fur, then kindly explain to the person who gave it to you why you won't be wearing it.

   c. Remove the collar and wear it without.

4. Animals in circuses and zoos often live:

   a. A lot longer than they would in the wild.

   b. In cramped enclosures, nothing like their natural environment.

   c. Shorter lives than their wild relatives because of the stress, disease, loneliness, and boredom they suffer.

Answers: 1. b; 2. a—but c is also a great idea!; 3. if you've read Chapter 8, your answer better be b!; 4. both b and c are correct

Did You Know?

🐾 When she was 13, Shawna Christine Hendrix let people know about Iams' cruel "nutrition" tests on animals by making her own Iams flyer with information that she downloaded from PETA's Web site. Then she hit the pet-food company where it hurts by posting the flyer on bulletin boards in stores that sell Iams.

🐾 Heather Hermann, from Denver, circulated a petition and gathered 6,000 signatures in order to put an initiative banning wild animal acts to the vote in the city's election. "In the wild, bears are not riding bicycles, and tigers are not jumping through hoops of fire," Heather told a reporter for the Associated Press. The story on Heather's awesome achieve-ment was printed in newspapers all over the country.

🐾 Robin Sawyer's stomach turned as her teacher announced her plans for Robin's fashion class: the teacher was going to take the class to visit a furrier. Robin didn't waste a second and logged onto PETA's Web site to get the nitty-gritty about how fur farmers suffocate minks and how trappers break their victims' necks to kill them. Robin schooled her teacher and class about the cruel fur industry, and her persistence paid off. They nixed plans to visit the furrier!

🐾 Actor Joaquin Phoenix's whole family stopped eating meat and all animal products after he and his brother, River, started asking their parents why they had to take animals' lives for food and what exactly went into hamburgers and hot dogs. Pretty soon their whole family started thinking about the an-swers to those questions and decided to go vegetarian.

What You Can Do

🐾 Don't get mad! Others might wonder why you care so much about animals and might not share your feelings about pro-tecting them. Many people are taught to think of animals as nothing more than "things," but with patience and the facts, you can help them understand.

🐾 Don't get discouraged! Some people might feel uncomfortable when you talk about respecting animals instead of using them. Some might even try to make fun of you. Let them know that animals should be thought of as friends and it's weird not to care about them. Tell them that what's best for any animal is best for all animals, including us.

🐾 Don't give up! It might seem hard at times to make others understand why you refuse to cut up animals in biology class, why you won't wear animal skins, or why you don't want to eat your friends. People have used animals for food, clothing, and entertainment for centuries, but just because something is a tradition doesn't mean it's right. Remember, slavery was once an accepted tradition in the United States and other countries. It takes time to help people change attitudes. Think of people who have struggled (and won), or are still struggling, to gain their freedom and rights. When humans band together, they can make wonderfully positive changes. If we work together for animals (that is, all animals—other-than-human beings and people), we'll have a much better world.

Check It Out

- If you need information on activities to help animals and ideas on how to get others involved in animal protection, you can write to PETA (501 Front St., Norfolk, VA 23510) and ask them to send you *Grrr!*, PETA's magazine for kids. Every four months you'll receive an issue full of facts that will help you get the word out to others about animal rights, and help your friends and family understand your commitment to protecting animals. For more information see www.petakids.com.

- You can subscribe to *Otterwise*, a quarterly newsletter "for kids who love animals." For more information, write to P.O. Box 1374, Portland, ME 04104.

- Write for a free information pack from Animal Aid Youth Group. They offer lots of advice and support—mainly for British kids, ages twelve to eighteen—but they would love to hear from you, too. Visit www.animalaid.org.uk/youth, write to the Old Chapel, Bradford St., Tonbridge, Kent TN9 1AW, UK.

CHAPTER 50

One Last Thing You Can Do to Help the Animals

When you have finished this book, please consider passing it on to a friend or giving it to your local library. That way many others will learn how to join you in saving the animals. Don't forget to tell us about anything you're doing to help animals. Send an e-mail to education@peta.org. Thank you, and good luck!

APPENDIX
A

Recipes for Kids Who Care

Here are a handful of delicious, easy-to-make recipes. For starters, try one contributed by Alicia Silverstone, who's not just a star in films—she rocks the kitchen too!

Alicia Silverstone's Steamy Creamy Artichoke Dip

2 8.5-oz. cans of quartered artichokes
1 cup vegan mayonnaise (such as Nayonaise)
1 cup soy parmesan "cheese"
1 tsp. paprika
Garlic powder, to taste

Preheat oven to 350°F. Drain the liquid from the artichokes, mash, and combine with other ingredients. Scoop into a casserole dish and bake for ½ hour. Sprinkle paprika on top before serving. Serve with chips, toasted and cut pita bread, or sliced fresh vegetables.

Super-Easy "Cheezy" Ramen

1 pkg. Top Ramen Oriental Noodle Soup
½ scoop nutritional yeast

Cook the noodles according to the directions on the package. Add the flavor packet and the nutritional yeast and stir.

Makes 1 serving.

Mango Creamsicle-Like Smoothie

1 mango, cut into pieces and frozen
½ cup pineapple chunks
⅓ cup vanilla soy milk
⅓ cup mango-pineapple fruit juice
1 scoop vanilla soy-protein powder
Couple ice cubes

Put all the ingredients in a blender and mix until creamy.

Makes 2 smoothies.

Chocolate Peanut-Butter Fudge

6 oz. (1 cup) semisweet chocolate chips
¼ cup brown sugar
2 tbsps. vanilla soy milk
½ cup oatmeal
⅓ cup natural peanut butter at room temperature

Combine the chocolate, sugar, and soy milk in the top of a double boiler or in a small aluminum bowl set on top of a saucepan filled with 2 inches of water. Cook over low heat until smoothly melted. Stir in the oatmeal. Then drop in the peanut butter by teaspoonfuls. Swirl it in until evenly distributed but not blended in. Line a small, shallow baking dish with wax paper. Pour in the mixture with the help of a rubber spatula. Refrigerate for at least 4 hours until firm, then cut into squares.

Easy Nachos

1 can black beans
1 cup salsa
¼ cup nutritional yeast
1 bag tortilla chips

1–2 diced tomatoes
½ cup chopped cilantro
2–3 diced green onions

Drain and heat the black beans.

Mix the salsa and the nutritional yeast in a separate, small container and heat.

Arrange the chips on a plate and top with the beans, salsa-yeast mixture, chopped tomatoes, cilantro, and onions.

Makes 4 to 6 servings.

Chocolate Banana Pudding

1 banana
2 cups soft silken tofu
⅓ cup cocoa powder
⅓ cup sugar

Throw everything into a food processor and blend until smooth.

Chill and serve.

It's also great for dipping strawberries!

Makes 4 servings.

Chunky Monkey Soy Shake

1 cup soy milk
1 banana
1 tbsp. sweetened chocolate powder
2 tbsp. roasted cashews

Pour the soy milk into the blender, then add the rest of the ingredients.

Blend until creamy.

Makes 1 shake.

Vegan Grilled Cheese

2 Tofutti cheddar slices
2 slices bread
Margarine

Put both slices of cheese on one slice of bread and cover it with the other slice. Spread the margarine on the outside of each slice of bread and heat in a pan until the cheese is melted and the bread is browned.

Makes 1 sandwich.

Hummus

1 15-oz. can chickpeas, rinsed and drained
3 garlic cloves, minced
1/3 cup tahini
1/4 cup fresh lemon juice
1/4 cup water
3/4 tsp. salt

Process the chickpeas in a food processor until smooth, stopping to scrape down the sides. Add the garlic and remaining ingredients. Pulse until blended.

Makes approximately 4 cups.

Yummy Creamy Salsa

3 tbsp. Tofutti Better Than Cream Cheese
1 cup salsa

Mix the ingredients together and enjoy with some nacho chips or veggies.

Makes 1 cup.

Vegan Peanut Butter Granola Mix

1 cup pretzel sticks, broken in half
1 cup raisins
1 cup Nature Valley Crunchy Peanut Butter Granola Bars, crumbled into small pieces
1/2 cup sunflower kernels

Combine all ingredients into a gallon-size plastic bag and shake until completely mixed.

Makes 3 1/2 cups.

Boca LT

1 Boca Burger
2 slices whole-wheat bread
Vegan mayo, to taste
Few pieces lettuce
Few slices tomato

Heat the Boca Burger in a pan and toast the bread. Spread mayo on the bread, add lettuce and tomato.

Makes 1 sandwich.

Mock Tuna Salad

4 cups garbanzo beans, cooked and drained
1 cup celery, finely chopped
1/2 cup onion, finely chopped
1–2 tbsp. nutritional yeast flakes
Vinegar-free pickle relish, to taste (optional)
Sea salt, to taste
Egg-free mayonnaise, to taste

Mix together all the ingredients except the egg-free mayonnaise, mashing the garbanzos slightly as you mix. Add the "mayonnaise" until the salad is as moist as you like.

Veggie Chicken Salad

1 package veggie chicken
1 small jar veggie mayo
Pickles, diced
Black pepper, to taste
Pita pocket shells

Dice the veggie chicken into small pieces. Add some mayo and a few diced pickles and lightly sprinkle with pepper. Mix it all up and let chill. Then grab the pita pocket shells and fill with veggie chicken salad mixture.

Makes 3 to 4 servings.

Falafel Nuggets

1 cup falafel mix
¾ cup hot water
Canola or olive oil

Mix the falafel mix with the hot water and let sit for 15 minutes. Heat some canola or olive oil in a skillet and shape the falafel into small, nugget-sized patties. Fry on each side until golden brown. Serve with your favorite sauce.

Makes 3 to 4 servings.

Spicy Vegan Pizza Bagels

1 bagel
1 small can tomato sauce
Hot sauce, to taste
Garlic salt, to taste
Shredded vegan mozzarella "cheese"
Veggies (optional)

Slice the bagel in half and spread the desired amount of sauce on each piece. Add a few drops of hot sauce to the tomato sauce and sprinkle with garlic salt. Add the "cheese" and veggies, if desired, put in a toaster oven, and heat until the cheese melts, or just enough to warm it up. For a milder version, omit the hot sauce.

Makes 1 serving.

Chocolate Chip Peanut Butter Waffle Sandwich

2 vegan waffles
Vegan chocolate chips, to taste
Peanut butter, to taste
Maple syrup, to taste

Toast the waffles lightly so that they're not burned. Put them on a plate and spread the desired amount of chocolate chips on the waffles and microwave them for about 3 seconds. Allow the chocolate chips to cool, then smear peanut butter on both waffles, smash them together, and top them off with a few squeezes of maple syrup. Voilà!

Makes 1 serving.

APPENDIX B

Tasty Vegan Foods to Try

All of these products are totally kind to the animals and good for you too. The best thing is, most of them can be found at your local grocery store. And don't forget the Silk Soy Nog! That's a totally delicious egg and milk-free "egg nog" made by the Silk soy milk company. Happy eating!

Vegan "Meats"

Boca

   Chick'n Nuggets
   Chick'n Patties
   Meatless Chili
   Roasted Garlic Burger
   Roasted Onion Burger
   Spicy Chick'n Patties
   Vegan Burger

Field Roast

   Original Field Roast Loaf
   Celebration Roast
   Thin Sliced Field Roast
   Field Roast Cutlets
   Field Roast Sausages
   Classic Meatloaf
   BBQ Field Roast

Gardenburger

Veggie Medley Burger
Black Bean Burger
GardenVegan Burger
Flame Grilled Burger
Homestyle Classic Burger
Meatless Flame Grilled Chicken
Meatless BBQ Chicken
Meatless Riblets
Meatless Buffalo Chicken Wings

Lightlife

Meatless Meatballs
Breakfast Patties
Burgers
Smart Links Country Sausage
Smart Bacon
Smart Ground Original
Smart Ground Taco & Burrito
Light Burgers
Smart Dogs
Smart Dogs Jumbo
Tofu Pups
Gimme Lean! Sausage Style
Gimme Lean! Ground Beef Style

Smart Deli

Roast Turkey Style
Country Ham Style
Old World Bologna
Three Peppercorn Pastrami Style
Pepperoni Slices

Morningstar Farms

Vegan Grillers
Meal Starters Chik'n Strips and Steak Strips
Vegan Sausage Links

Melissa's

Soy Ground
Soy Taco
Soyrizo

Now & Zen

UnTurkey
UnChicken
UnRibs

Sol Cuisine

Original Burger
Vegetable Burger
Sol-Dog
Jumbo Sol-Dog
Sol-Ground Original
Sol-Ground Tex-Mex
T-Ribz

Turtle Island Foods

Tofurky Deli Slices
    Original
    Peppered
    Hickory
    Cranberry & Stuffing
    Italian Deli
    "Philly Style" Steak
Tofurky Beer Brats

Tofurky Sweet Italian Sausages
Tofurky Kielbasa
SuperBurgers
   Original
   Smoked
   TexMex
Tofurky Feast
Tofurky Roast

Yves

Canadian Veggie Bacon
Garden Vegetable Patties
Hot 'n' Spicy Chili Veggie Dogs
The Good Dog
Original Jumbo Veggie Dogs
Santa Fe Veggie Beef
Thai Lemongrass Veggie Chick'n
The Good Veggie Burger
Tofu Dogs
Veggie "Neatballs"
Veggie Bologna Slices
Veggie Breakfast Links
Veggie Breakfast Patties
Veggie Chick'n Burgers
Veggie Chick'n Nuggets
Veggie Dogs
Veggie Ground Round Italian
Veggie Ground Round Mexican
Veggie Ground Round Original
Veggie Ham Slices
Veggie Lasagna
Veggie Pizza Pepperoni
Veggie Salami Slices
Veggie Turkey Slices

Vegi-Deli

> Vegi Deli Salami
> Vegi Deli Pepperoni

Worthington

> Tuno
> Chickette

Vegan Ice Creams

Rice Dream Non-Dairy Frozen Desserts

> Vanilla
> Orange Vanilla Swirl
> Cappuccino
> Cappuccino Almond Fudge Supreme
> Carob
> Carob Almond
> Chocolate
> Cocoa Marble Fudge
> Pralines 'N Dream Supreme
> Strawberry
> Neapolitan
> Cherry Vanilla

Soy Dream Non-Dairy Frozen Desserts

> French Vanilla
> Green Tea
> Butter Pecan
> Strawberry Swirl
> Mocha Fudge
> Vanilla Fudge Swirl
> Soy Dream Lil' Dreamers
> Vanilla
> Chocolate

Tea Dreams Frozen Non-Dairy Desserts

Chocolate Caramel Chai
Cinnamon Apple Spice
Imperial White Peach
Tropic of Srawberry
Vanilla Ginger Spice Chai
Vanilla Hazelnut

Tofutti

Sticks

Marry Me Bars
Totally Fudge Pops
Chocolate Fudge Treats
Delights
Monkey Bars
Hooray Hooray
Coffee Break Treats

Tofutti Cuties

Blueberry Wave
Chocolate
Chocolate Wave
Coffee Break
Cookies 'N Cream
Jazzy
Mint Chocolate Chip
No Sugar Vanilla
Peanut Butter
Strawberry Wave
Totally Vanilla
Vanilla
Wild Berry

Tofutti Too Too's

Vanilla Chocolate Chip

Tofutti Kids

Lime
Orange
Strawberry

Tofutti No-Sugar-Added Pints

Strawberry
Chocolate

Tofutti Pints

Better Pecan
Chocolate Cookie Crunch
Chocolate Supreme
Mint Chocolate Chip
Vanilla Almond Bark
Vanilla Fudge
Vanilla
Wildberry Supreme

Tofutti Low-Fat Pints

Chocolate Fudge
Coffee Marshmallow Swirl
Vanilla Fudge

Super Soy Supreme Pints

Bella Vanilla
New York, New York Chocolate

Cheesecake Supreme Pints

Chocolate Cheesecake Supreme
Strawberry Cheesecake Supreme
Blueberry Cheesecake Supreme

Soy Delicious

Sweet Nothings

Fudge Bar
Mango Raspberry

Carb Escapes

Butter Pecan
Chocolate
Chocolate Almond
Chocolate Peanut Butter
Mint Chip
Strawberry
White Mousse

It's Soy Delicious Pints

Almond Pecan
Awesome Chocolate
Black Leopard
Carob Peppermint
Chocolate Almond
Chocolate Peanut Butter
Espresso
Green Tea
Mango Raspberry
Pistachio Almond
Raspberry
Tiger Chai
Vanilla
Vanilla Fudge

Purely Decadent Pints

Cherry Nirvana
Chocolate Brownie Almond

Chocolate Obsession
Chunky Mint Madness
Cookie Avalanche
Mint Chocolate Chip
Mocha Almond Fudge
Peanut Butter Zig Zag
Praline Pecan
Purely Vanilla
Raspberry À La Mode
Rocky Road
Swinging Anna Banana
Turtle Trails
Vanilla Swiss Almond

Chicago Soy Dairy Temptation

Chocolate Chip Cookie Dough
Fair Trade Organic Chocolate
French Vanilla
Peach Cobbler
Mint Chocolate Chip

Vegan Ready-Made Meals

Amy's

Asian Noodle Stir-Fry
Bean & Rice Burrito–Non Dairy
Breakfast Burrito
Black Bean Vegetable Burrito
Thai Stir-Fry
Teriyaki Bowl
Brown Rice & Vegetables Bowl
Brown Rice, Black-Eyed Peas & Veggies Bowl
Light in Sodium Brown Rice & Veggies Bowl
Tofu Scramble

Indian Samosa Wraps
Indian Mattar Tofu
Indian Vegetable Korma
Black Bean Vegetable Enchilada
Family-Size Black Bean Vegetable Enchilada
Light in Sodium Black Bean Enchilada
Enchilada With Spanish Rice and Beans
Black Bean Enchilada Whole Meal
Non-Dairy Vegetable Pot Pie
Roasted Vegetable Pizza
Mexican Tamale Pie
Shepherd's Pie
Spicy Chili

Fantastic Foods

Vegetarian Spanish Paella
Vegetarian Thai Lemon Grass
Vegetarian Pad Thai
Vegetarian 3-Bean Chili

Gardenburger

Meatloaf with Broccoli & Red Peppers Meal
Citrus Glazed Chicken with Green Beans & Rice Meal
Southwestern Chicken with Vegetables Meal
Sweet & Sour Pork with Rice Meal

Lightlife

Smart BBQ
Smart Chili
Smart Tex-Mex
Smart Menu Orange Sesame Chick'n
Smart Menu Garlic Teriyaki Chick'n
Smart Tortilla Wrap Chick'n Rancher

Moosewood

> Hearty Mushroom Barley Soup
> Mediterranean Tomato & Rice Soup
> Moroccan Stew
> Pasta e Fagioli
> Spicy Penne Puttanesca
> Texas Two Bean Chili
> Tuscan White Bean & Vegetable Soup

Tasty Bite

> Spinach Dal & Basmati Rice
> Bombay Potatoes
> Punjab Eggplant
> Bengal Lentils

Yves

> Veggie Chili
> Veggie Lasagna
> Thai Lemongrass Veggie Chick'n
> Veggie Penne
> Sante Fe Veggie Beef

If that's not enough to convince you, there's also loads of yummy products that are "accidentally" vegan and totally safe for you to eat, so always check the ingredients before counting anything out. Here's just a few examples, which are probably already old favorites:

> All-Bran
> Apple Cinnamon Cheerios
> Apple Jacks
> Berry Burst Cheerios
> Cap'n Crunch Peanut Butter Crunch
> Cheerios
> Cinnamon Crunch Crispix

Cocoa Pebbles
Cocoa Rice Krispies
Corn Flakes
Cracklin' Oat Bran
Crispix
Fruit Loops
Grape Nuts
Just Right
Nature's Valley Granola Bars (Brown Sugar)
Pop Tarts
Raisin Bran
Ghirardelli Hot Chocolate (Chocolate Hazelnut)
Ghirardelli Hot Chocolate (Chocolate Mocha)
Ghirardelli Hot Chocolate (Double Chocolate)
Hershey Syrup
Nestlé Nesquick Syrup
Airheads Taffy
Anna's Almond Cinnamon Thins
Anna's Ginger Thins
Archway Ginger Snaps
Blow Pops
Brownstone Baking Co. Mini Bagel Crisps (Garlic)
Chocolove Dark Chocolate bar
Cry Babies
Dem Bones
Dots
Dum Dums
Entenmann's Fudge Delights Fudge & Mint Cookies
Famous Amos Sandwich Cookies
Fireballs
Fritos (Barbecue)
Grandma's Peanut Butter Sandwich Cremes
Hubba Bubba Bubblegum
Jujubees
Jujufruits
Keebler Animal Crackers

Kool-Aid Gels
Krispy Kreme Fruit Pies
Laffy Taffy
Lance Nut-O Lunch Cookies (Peanut Butter)
Lance Nut-O Lunch Cookies (Strawberry Creme)
Lay's Potato Chips (Natural Country Barbecue)
Nabisco Uh-oh Oreos, Spring Oreos, and Chocolate Creme Oreos
Nutter Butter Bites
Panda Licorice
PezRing pop lollipops
Skittles' Mints
Smarties (U.S. version only)
Sour Patch Kids
Starburst (jelly beans and hard candy)
Betty Crocker Bac*O's Bacon Flavor Bits
McCormick Bac'n Pieces
Safeway Whipped Cream (canned)
Smuckers Uncrustables Peanut Butter and Grape Jelly
Smuckers Uncrustables Peanut Butter and Strawberry Jam
Betty Crocker Bisquick
Ghirardelli Chocolate Chip Cookie Mix
Green Giant Cream Style Sweet Corn
Jello-O Instant Pudding
Thai Kitchen Noodle Bowls (Thai Peanut, Roasted Garlic, Lemon-
    grass & Chili, and Pad Thai)
Tropical Source Dark Chocolate Chips
Uncle Ben's Cinnamon and Raisin Rice Pudding Mix